Jim Mindling has a great [...]
many Christians face too[...]
creative, insightful, reflective resource on understanding how
to cooperate with God as He transforms us into the image
of His Son. This book is fun to read, well-written, inspiring
and right on target. Many people try to shed new light on
old issues, but Jim has definitely succeeded here. You will find
this book not only helpful and challenging, but also easy to
implement if you are willing. I dare you to put into practice
the simple truths contained in this book and I guarantee that
if you do, you will love the results.

DR. TOM BLACKABY
Author, speaker, International Director
for Blackaby Ministries International.

This is a book about living life more abundantly. Jim Mindling
has devoted many years to understanding spiritual breathing
as an indispensable foundation for every believer. By carefully
observing Jesus' character, patterns and practices, Jim has
captured the essence of the Spirit-filled life. Learn to Breathe
may be your personal key to experiencing the vibrant joy of
the Holy Spirit's presence and power in your daily walk.

JOHN D. BECKETT
Chairman, The Beckett Companies
Author, Loving Monday and Mastering Monday

This is a great book! Learn to Breathe is a biblically based
work, drawing extensively from the Scriptures. It is a practical
book, using moving illustrations to make important everyday
life applications. God's highest goal for us is that we become

like Christ. If we embrace that goal for our lives, then this book will be a means of grace the Holy Spirit will use to facilitate that transformation.

DR. JERRY D. PORTER
General Superintendent Church of the Nazarene

Learn to Breathe is a means of grace. Jim's fresh and practical approach to unpacking the workings of God, by means of His Spirit, to bring about ongoing, genuine transformation into the likeness of Christ is a gift to both individual believers and the church collectively.

JOEL ATWELL
Senior Pastor
Grace Community Church

Extending the approach of Dallas Willard, Mindling offers up an evangelical approach to spiritual formation that not only draws deeply from his years of pastoral experience, but—and this is a real strength of the book—also from brutally honest reflections on his own journey of attempting to cooperate with the Spirit's forming Christ in him. Combining a pastor's passion to see Christ formed in his people with a quick wit and an engaging style of writing, he not only encourages his readers toward living cruciform, surrendered lives of love for God and for others, he concretely shows them how to cooperate with the Spirit's transformative work in their lives. His controlling metaphor of breathing in God's empowering, transforming Spirit and breathing out the toxins that inhibit God's work in transforming us into the image of Jesus is fleshed out in numerous practical, day-to-day practices through which not only individuals are transformed but whole churches as well. It is a pleasure to recommend this book from the pen of a gifted pastor who also happens to be one of my best friends, one in whom I've seen the image of Jesus continuously being formed for almost thirty years.

DR. ANDY JOHNSON
Professor of New Testament
Nazarene Theological Seminary

This book provides refreshing winds of the Spirit and brings us to the reality of how the Holy Spirit is our helper in Spiritual Formation and becoming more like Christ in our daily walk.

DR. DALE GALLOWAY
Best Selling Author, Leading with
Vision and On Purpose Leadership

In this book Jim Mindling invites you to ponder anew what breathing in the life of the Spirit can mean in your Christian walk of faith. He offers a theological framework with practical applications to help disciples of Christ move from the shallow breathing that leaves us weary to the deep breathing of an abundant life. All of us need to be continually challenged to know there is more that God wants to do in us and through us. This book is a great voice of challenge to fully enter the great adventure of life with God.

DR. MARY REARICK PAUL
Vice-President for Spiritual Development
Point Loma Nazarene University

Learn
to
Breathe

The Surprising Path to
a Transformed Life

....

J I M   M I N D L I N G

....

WESTBOW
P R E S S
A DIVISION OF THOMAS NELSON

WestBow Press books may be ordered through booksellers or by contacting:

WestBow Press
A Division of Thomas Nelson
1663 Liberty Drive
Bloomington, IN 47403
www.westbowpress.com
1-(866) 928-1240

Cover design: David Swidrak

ISBN: 978-1-4497-9353-1 (sc)
ISBN: 978-1-4497-9354-8 (hc)
ISBN: 978-1-4497-9352-4 (e)

Library of Congress Control Number: 2013907665

Printed in the United States of America.

WestBow Press rev. date: 01/21/2014

TABLE OF CONTENTS

• •

Acknowledgements

· ·

My greatest thanks go to the persons of the Trinity. God the Father, You have loved me with an everlasting love and poured out Your grace to me beyond measure. Jesus, thank You for loving me, dying on the cross for me and showing me how to live full of and led by the Holy Spirit. I want to be more like You more than anything in this world. Holy Spirit, thank You for filling me, gracing me, empowering me, breathing new life into me and for all You've done to seek to transform me to the image of Christ.

To all of those who have loved and graced me, starting with my parents and siblings, Jim and Pat, Jane, Tim, John and Leslie, your formative influence still impacts me after all these years. Thank you for being a remarkable family of unconditional love.

I have pastored four churches and have dearly loved the people of each one. Each church has taught me so much about becoming like Christ and helped me grow as a pastor, teacher, leader and disciple: Norristown Church of the Nazarene, New Community Church of the Nazarene, CrossWinds Community Church and Church of the Open Door. Thank you for loving me, listening to me, and being caught up in the same vision that has captured my heart all these years: the church becoming more like Christ to the glory of God.

John Beckett, your wisdom, generosity and loving advice have been an incredible encouragement to me.

JoAnn Keesor, Michelle Eddy, Ken Rhodes, Norma Lambert, Angie Kiesling, Jamie Jackson, Dan Samms, Cindy Bublinec, Ben Fowlkes, Dave Mooibroek, Jan Caughlin, David Swidrak, you have all provided help on different stages of the manuscript, design, and/or roll out. Thank you so much.

I have a long list of friends who have prayed for me, helped me, encouraged me and/or constantly asked me for updates about the book: the awesome staff of Church of the Open Door, I love doing ministry with you; Lynnette Scott, Paul Mallasch, Robby and Norri Robinson, Carlee Goodall, Marge Oyster, Andy Johnson, Roger and Linda Tenney, Judi Fischer, Chantal Dalencour, Alan Schafer, Jack Parker, Henry Miner, Darrell Dunckel, Case and Vi Mooibroek, Jason Russ, Larry and Ruth Russ, Brian Johnson, Melvin and Carmen Hunt, Jeff and Patti Leimgruber, Randy and Debbie Helland, Mike and Jan Gargasz, Greg and Terry Hogan, Phyllis Garcia, Ken and Mary Houston, Dan and Kim Bieri, David and Ashley Abraham, Keith and Carol Klekota, Dave and Jeanie Williams.

To all of those who prayed for this book and for me without telling me, thank you.

No one on this earth has encouraged me in writing this book more than my wife Andrea. Sometimes cheering, sometimes prodding, patiently listening to and reading thousands of editable words, you kept encouraging me to stay at it and get it done. Your ideas, feedback, suggestions, advice and support have been invaluable. We're better together. I love you and am so grateful to you.

Likewise, no one has had a greater impact on helping me learn what it means to become more like Christ than Andrea and our four kids: Ryan, Caylie, Christa, and Julianna. No one has seen more of my failure to be like Christ and been hurt more from my lack of Christlikeness. But no one has loved me through it all as much as you. You, I love.

INTRODUCTION

What if I told you that learning a new way to breathe is the only way to fulfill your purpose in life?

If you've ever been in the room with a woman who was in the agonizing throes of delivering a baby, then you know making the statement, "You just need to breathe!" could be dangerous. One might need to duck or take a step back after giving such advice. However, for the person who puts those words into practice, the result is new life.

It's not just *that* you breathe; it's *how* you breathe that makes the difference.

The surprising truth is that this is true for you and me just as much as it is true for a woman experiencing excruciating labor pains. Really? Who needs to be told to do something they are already doing every second of the day?

I do.

And I'm guessing so do you.

But again, it's not just *that* you breathe, it's *how* you breathe that makes the difference.

We need to learn to breathe.

Elite runners, swimmers, weightlifters, women who've delivered babies, and *people who have an incredible, vibrant relationship with God* all have something in common: they've all discovered that breathing needs to be learned.

How you breathe makes all the difference between thriving or just surviving, between winning and losing, even between life and death.

But this kind of breathing has to be learned.

In fact, you can't fulfill your purpose in life until you learn a new way of breathing.

I'm not referring to a new technique of inhaling oxygen and exhaling carbon dioxide; I'm using breathing as a metaphor. This is not a literary metaphor; it's a life metaphor, a core foundational picture of how God designed us to live our lives.

What if God made us in such a way that how we breathe to sustain ourselves physically is a parallel to how we sustain ourselves spiritually? What if there was such a thing called Spiritual Breathing?

If this sounds like something you've heard from some New Age guru, let me clarify right up front that the ideas in this book are *not* some New Age philosophy but instead are centered on and drawn from the historic, orthodox teaching of the Bible, the Word of God. I am not teaching some ethereal, abstract spiritual breathing that makes you into a god or helps you become one with the universe.

As we will see in detail later in the book, the Bible teaches that the Holy Spirit is literally the *Breath of God* and we can learn to live our lives in an ongoing rhythm of repeatedly and continually "being filled with the Spirit" (Eph. 5:18) as we practice *biblical* Spiritual Breathing.

Job 33:4 says, "The Spirit of God has made me; the breath of the Almighty gives me life." The Spirit of God ALWAYS leads us to Jesus Christ. In fact, the truest test of whether you are being filled with and led by the Holy Spirit—instead of some other "spirit"—always comes down to whether or not you are becoming more like Christ.

And that, my friends, is the overriding purpose of your life! The purpose of your life is to become like Christ.

Most people aren't even aware that the purpose of life is to become like Christ. Others sense there's more to life, but don't know how to make it happen.

The key to becoming like Christ is discovering how to cooperate with the work of the Holy Spirit—learning the rhythm of breathing in His life-giving presence and breathing out the toxins that poison our soul. The only way to live the Christlike life is to keep receiving a fresh infilling of the renewing, forgiving, strengthening, sanctifying presence of the Holy Spirit.

We need to learn to breathe.

When you're being tempted, you need to breathe.

When you've been mistreated or hurt, you need to breathe.

When someone asks you to pray for them, you need to breathe.

When you're discouraged, you need to breathe.

When you read your Bible, you need to breathe.

When God convicts you of sin, you need to breathe.

When God opens an opportunity to share your faith, you need to breathe.

When you are confused, angry, or anxious, you need to breathe.

When you feel...okay, I think you get the idea.

I am shocked at how long it took me to learn how to breathe. After reading thousands of pages of books, earning a doctoral degree, studying, listening, reflecting, thinking, writing, teaching, praying with and helping hundreds of individuals personally grow in their faith, I've learned a lot. But as much as I've learned through classical education and helping people, I've learned even more in failing, struggling, repenting, loving, praying, receiving grace, and learning to breathe the Breath of God into my own life. God has led me on an adventure of biblical proportions!

I believe there are millions of Christ-followers who have plateaued and desire to grow spiritually but are uncertain how to go to the next level. I wrote this book to help us learn how to cooperate with what the Spirit of God is doing. The

Holy Spirit is seeking to make a holy people, and the essence of holiness is Christlikeness.

Section One casts the vision for Christlikeness and "Spiritual Breathing" then includes a review of the person and work of the Holy Spirit. Sections Two-Four explore the Six Core Christlike Characteristics produced in the life of Jesus of Nazareth as He cooperated with the work of the Holy Spirit. Each characteristic is applied and illustrated for today, giving the reader a practical, biblical curriculum for Christlikeness.

Learning to practice Spiritual Breathing is the key to becoming like Christ, so at the end of each of the chapters on the Core Christlike Characteristics, there is a Breathing Example and some Breathing Exercises to help us.

We were created to become like Christ.

We just need to learn to breathe.

So, if you're not in a delivery room, turn the page.

Becoming Like Christ

. . . .

CHAPTER ONE

Breathless

I was dying and I knew it. Everything in me strained to take a breath. My heart was beating faster, but my lungs wouldn't cooperate. Desperately, I tried again and again to breathe, each attempt a terrifying failure. Pinned to the ground by fear and helplessness, I was suffocating with my mouth wide open. Although only in the third grade, I was old enough to know what dying felt like. What started out to be some harmless disobedience suddenly became the most terrifying moment in my short life.

Living on a farm in southern Ohio and itching for some adventure, I was trying to figure out a way to ride a horse that my parents specifically had told me not to try to ride. Since I was so small that I couldn't get a saddle on the horse, let alone reach a stirrup, I led her over to a fence, tied her up, and scampered up to the top rail.

The plan was simple: jump off the fence onto the horse. Poised on the rail just before my jump, I congratulated myself for beating the system. This was going to be the ride of my life. I don't think anybody had ever tried jumping onto this horse from the fence, and she wasn't expecting it, so when I landed on her back with a thump she panicked.

The next thing I knew I was airborne in the barnyard and landing on the ground smack on my back. The impact knocked the breath right out of me. As I lay on the ground gasping for air, my mind was dominated by one thought: I just need to breathe!

I doubt if I had ever thought of breathing until that point in my life, and now that I couldn't breathe it was the only thing I could think about. At that moment, breathing was the most critical thing in my life. I was dying, alone, with no one to help me. Panic-stricken and helpless, my life passed before my eyes, all eight years of it. Sprawled out in the barnyard I made desperate promises to God about obeying my parents. I vowed to return the five-dollar bill I had stolen from my mother's purse. I would even be nice to my sister, anything—I was willing to do whatever it took to meet the greatest need of my life: I just need to breathe!

And then it happened. Just as suddenly as I had stopped breathing, I started breathing again. From death to life.

Apparently no one dies from getting the breath knocked out of them, but those who have experienced it will tell you they felt like they were going to die. Why? Because you can't breathe—at least you don't think you can. And, after all, *the only way to live is to breathe.* That's how important breath is. It is the basis of life itself, the gift of God.

Breathing is the central action in all of life. We do it without thinking. But while everyone already knows how to do this central *action* in life, very few people apply it to the central *area* of life.

It is humbling to admit that though I have earned three advanced degrees and have been in the people-helping business for over twenty years, I can't think of anything I've learned that has more power to change your life and our world than what I discovered in those desperate moments lying in the barnyard. Of course, I didn't realize it then; it took me several decades to discover the life-transforming truths latent in that simple phrase: I just need to breathe.

What if embedded in this most basic of life principles God has given us the secret to living the life He dreamed for us and that we so desperately long to live? What if God made us in such a way that how we breathe to sustain ourselves physically is a parallel to how we are sustained spiritually?

Ever since Christians have reflected on how to live the Christian life, a small but steady number of them have discovered this secret of living in rhythm with God. Some of these spiritual giants have left books, journals, or other writings that describe this rhythm. But far too many Christians never learn these truths, and their disappointing lives bear it out. Each generation needs to rediscover these simple but powerful truths. Not only is this basic life principle the secret to spiritual growth, it is the key to your ability to fulfill the purpose for which God created you.

This book is about taking something we already know how to do in one area of our life and learning how to extend it to the most important part of our life. What is true for our physical body is true for our spiritual life: the only way to live is to breathe.

The Breath of Life

When God made the first man, Genesis 2:7 says that God "breathed into his nostrils the *breath of life*, and the man

5

became a living being" (italics added). Until God breathed into him this life-giving breath, Adam was just a stiff carcass lying there on the ground or propped up against a tree looking like a mannequin in the storage room of a clothing store. He had a body but no life. The breath gave him life. Job 14:10 provides the bookend: "But man dies and is laid low; he *breathes his last* and is no more" (italics added). Put simply: you breathe, you live. When you stop breathing, you die. This is true both physically and spiritually. The abundant life God intended for us to live can be sustained only as we learn and practice "Spiritual Breathing."

Breathing is not the *goal* of life, but no one reaches his or her goal apart from breathing. Breathing makes reaching the goal possible. However, what is so obvious physically gets completely ignored by most of us spiritually. I know in my own life I was ignorant of this powerful but simple truth for years and years. Sometimes the most profound things are as close as the air we breathe.

Maybe this has happened to you too. There was a time in your life when you were living for God, excited about what God had done in your life and eager to know Him and grow as a Christian. It may have been when you were a teenager or a young adult or perhaps later in life. There was a hunger to know God and to live for Him, and life was an adventure. You took your first "breaths" as a young Christian, and your goal was to grow in the Lord. You may not have even realized that as you grew as a Christian you were beginning the process of "growing in every way more and more like Christ" (Ephesians 4:15 NLT), but you were. You were on the right track.

God's Purpose for Your Life

Just as when you were born physically, breathing without thinking about it, so as you started your Christian life you began the process of what Bill Bright called "Spiritual Breathing." You confessed (breathed "out") your sin and received (breathed "in") the life-giving Spirit of God, who applied forgiveness to your heart. You recognized your need for God, breathed in His Spirit, and received just what you needed to live.

God by His Spirit was at work in you, beginning to fulfill His purpose in your life, which is for you to "become like his Son" (Romans 8:28-29). Yes, God's goal when He created you was for you to be like Christ. He invited you on the adventure of a lifetime, the great adventure for which every human being is born. God wants you to grow and mature in the Christian life, cooperating with His grace and being led by His Spirit—that's the process of Christlikeness. And the only way to reach our goal of Christlikeness is by practicing Spiritual Breathing.

Remember this: the goal of the Christian life is to become like Christ. The only way to reach that goal is by practicing Spiritual Breathing, learning how to receive God's power and grace into your life on an ongoing basis.

This adventure of becoming like Christ is challenging, exciting, and filled with risk and intrigue. But it's not easy or predictable, and for many the goal of living for Christ and becoming more like Him gets sabotaged. Something happens and they get the breath knocked out of them. Their goal changes from living to merely surviving. It may have been sudden, like falling off a horse, or it may have been gradual the way spring changes to summer which gives way to fall and then winter. But whether it was sudden or gradual, something's changed.

I meet people all the time who've gotten the breath knocked out of them. They are desperately gasping for air, and they don't know what to do next. Like Mike and Alissa.

———•oo-◦❁◦-oo•———

Mike wouldn't have stood out in a crowd. He liked simple American food, drove a late-model Ford Taurus sedan, and lived in a modest home. As he left the restaurant that night with his family, he fumbled for his keys and tried to remember where he parked his silver Taurus. He clicked the fob on his key chain and followed the staccato tones of the car horn and the simultaneous flicker of the headlights to his car. *If only it was this easy to find a job*, he thought to himself with a sigh louder than he realized.

His wife, Alissa, responded to the sigh just in time to see in his eyes a virtual mirror of her own fatigue and fear. She started to say something but was too tired to fight. As they drove home, she gazed listlessly out the window.

The next thing she felt took her completely by surprise.

As they drove by the church where they were members, she strangely felt ambushed by a wave of loneliness. Christ Community Church was a good church full of nice people, but all of a sudden she felt completely isolated from the place she and Mike had attended for ten years. *I don't belong there*, she thought, shocked by the strength and abruptness of the emotion. *If the people there knew our situation, they'd turn their backs on us in a heartbeat.*

Quietly she broke into her own thoughts: "I don't want to go to church tomorrow." Her voice was faint enough that Mike didn't hear what she said but loud enough to jar him out of his post-pork chop daze.

"What?" he said.

She noticed the irritation in his tone but couldn't choke back the tears. "I don't want to go to church tomorrow!"

"What for?" Mike asked, meaning "why not?" while wondering where in the world all this was coming from.

"I don't feel like we're good enough for them," Alissa complained.

"Not good enough?!" Mike began to escalate into an angry flurry of defensiveness, guilt, and blame. Just as quickly, Alissa realized her mistake and was flooded with regret.

I set him off again, she mourned inwardly, worried what he might say in front of the kids slouching in the backseat. As Mike went into an autopilot rant, the swelling regret in Alissa swirled with irritated scorn as she replayed in her mind the neon message that blared from the church sign they had just passed: "Become more like Christ at Christ Community Church!" She despised the cheery, optimistic message because it served as a glaring reminder of just how un-Christlike she felt.

It wasn't that she hadn't tried to be more like Christ. Alissa had worked tirelessly at the church, teaching the threes and fours for the last nine years, serving on the budget finance council, and hosting a disciple group in her home every Wednesday night. The past five years in a row she had directed the children's Christmas program, vowing each year that it was her last. After another crazy fifty-plus-hour work week at the CPA firm, she desperately needed a weekend off.

She wanted to be a faithful follower of Jesus Christ, but at home she flew off the handle at the smallest thing and carried around exhausting residual guilt for constantly nagging Austin and Alise, her teenage kids. When she could, she squeezed in some time to read her Bible and pray, but prayer was usually reduced to reciting her shopping list of needs in the car on her way to work.

The pastor's latest series on discipleship just heaped more guilt on her. She had tried and tried to be more like Jesus, but her repeated failures seemed to make the whole idea of becoming like Christ totally unattainable.

"I could never be like Christ," she told herself. "I'm just not good enough; besides, my life is too crazy."

By now, Mike was in prime form as he worked his way down his mental list of other families who attended Christ Community, favorably comparing himself to each one and building his case for why they were just as good as any other family at the church.

"Oh, we're good enough," he fumed, "but I refuse to play that whole hypocritical game of thinking you can become like Christ. I mean, who are they kidding? Nobody can be like Christ. The whole thing is a sham. Besides, if they are so Christlike, we sure could use some help." He knew he wouldn't accept help from the church and would be horrified if they offered, but he convinced himself that his point was still valid.

Mike and Alissa's life was already hectic and their marriage strained. But the day Mike received the pink slip, it felt like he got the wind knocked out of him and he had never recovered. His passion for God and the church waned as his defensiveness and anger escalated. Alissa knew he was hurting, but Mike wouldn't talk about it. He honestly didn't know what to do. Johnson Supply was the only place he had ever worked, and nobody else was hiring. God was silent, and Mike seriously doubted whether He even noticed, let alone cared.

The men's group had been studying how God uses everyday life to make us more like Christ, and part of Mike missed being with the guys; but a stronger part of him was tired of the struggle. If becoming more like Christ was so biblical, why was it so hard? And how could God expect anybody to be like Christ anyway? It's like expecting someone to run a mile in thirty seconds, or pole vault over the Empire State Building. Why bother trying? Why wasn't it good enough to go to church, read your Bible, and be a nice person? Why did the bar have to be set so high? Was being like Christ really that important? Besides, what did it all have to do with selling auto parts and keeping your job?

Candidates for Christlikeness

Mike's questions are valid questions; Alissa's feelings are real and legitimate. Though not identical, their situation is similar to many others', maybe even yours. There seems to be a disconnect between the message of the Bible and their everyday lives. They see no relevance between the goal of the Christian life and their own life. Are they candidates for Christlikeness? If you could drill down to the bottom line they might summarize their questions like this:

1. What does becoming like Christ have to do with the real, everyday life I live?
2. If it's even possible to actually be like Christ, what does that mean?
3. How in the world does someone become like Christ?

Sadly, many Christians have not even heard the biblical call to Christlikeness. Explained away or ignored by preachers and teachers, coming to Christ is all they understand. Becoming *like* Christ for some reason never gets on their radar. But for the rest, when they hear the idea of becoming like Christ they usually respond in one of three ways:

- Christlikeness is a pipedream
- Christlikeness is an arrogant aspiration
- Christlikeness is just for spiritual superstars

Those who view becoming like Christ as nothing more than a pipedream might say, "Don't be ridiculous, it's unattainable. No one can ever be like Christ. Striving to be like Christ is an exercise in frustration." Some speak from the sense of failure of trying to be like Christ in their own strength. Others are simply unaware of what the Bible teaches. For whatever reason, these good people have resigned themselves to accept a watered-down version of

Deprived of essencial content ↑

salvation, an eviscerated gospel. They're like eagles that have been convinced they are penguins.

Other people hear about someone aspiring to be like Christ and end up accusing them of arrogance: "Wasn't that the very first temptation, thinking we could be like God? Weren't Satan's exact words to Eve that upon eating the fruit of the Tree of the Knowledge of Good and Evil she would 'be like God'?" "Isn't it arrogant and prideful to even think we could ever be like Christ?" These folks are confused and misinformed about what the Bible teaches, and for either defensive or argumentative reasons they conveniently dismiss one of the core teachings of the Bible. They're like the scientists who stood around with their arms crossed smoking their pipes, convinced that man could never fly while Orville and Wilbur Wright were out launching their latest wood, wire, and fabric contraption into the Atlantic coast wind.

Still others have convinced themselves that while it may be possible for some very spiritual people to become like Christ, it's definitely not for them. This third group is comprised of frustrated people tired of failing or those who, with every defeated step away from Christ, argue that it's not in their spiritual DNA. Whatever their excuse, these folks view Christlikeness as the major leagues: only the extremely gifted get in. Not everybody has the gifts of an elite athlete or the strengths of a Navy Seal. Some of us are just wired differently. There are only a few Billy Grahams and Mother Teresas in each generation.

There is a fourth category of people, and I hope you're in this group. If you're not right now, I hope you will be soon.

When these people hear about becoming like Christ, they're intrigued, even drawn to the thought. There is something that resonates deep inside them and says, *Yes, this is right. I want to be more like Jesus. Tell me more.* It is neither a sense of confidence in their own ability nor an ambition they have always had. It's more a sense of calling, a deep curiosity, an adventure.

This is a broad group of people of all ages and stages, a diverse collection of people united by a common thread: Jesus Christ has changed their lives, filled them with His Spirit, and they are seeking to cooperate with what He is doing in their lives. They're ordinary people envisioned by an extraordinary dream: fully realizing the God-given potential inside of them to walk in intimate relationship with the living God, to cooperate fully with His sanctifying work in their lives, and to be a part of His redemptive work in the world.

This is not a nameless mass of people conjured up for the purpose of illustration. These are real people with real names and real families and real issues. Many of them go to my church. Others are people I've met over the years. Some are from my family. They are under no illusions that they "have what it takes" to become like Christ in and of themselves, but they have responded with faith to what the Bible teaches and believe that God is at work in them to make them more and more like His Son. They are forgiven sinners of all ages and stages, men and women who are learning how to live surrendered to the loving leadership of the Spirit of God in their lives.

While their lives increasingly resemble Jesus Christ, they aren't perfect. They still know the <u>deceptive allure</u> <u>of entrenched self-centeredness</u>, but they have learned that when they fail, they can draw upon the grace of God and *<u>breathe in the renewing, life-giving presence of the Holy Spirit.</u>* These people are housewives, salesmen, students, executives, plumbers, accountants, clerks, secretaries, pastors, lawyers, assembly line workers, nurses, landscape architects, those with great jobs, those with boring jobs and those who have lost their jobs. They are everyday people who have responded to the call of the adventure of becoming like Christ. Filled with and led by the Spirit of God, together they form the Christlike church that is the hope of the world. They are people just like you and me, but they have learned the powerful secret of how to apply the most important action in life to the most important area of life.

Remember this: God by His Holy Spirit is working to make us more like Christ. We just need to breathe.

. . . .

CHAPTER TWO

I Want to Be Jesus Tonight

"**D**addy, I want to be Jesus tonight!" all three of my little girls squealed in unison when I walked into the room. I had promised them if everybody got ready for bed by 8:00, we would do a bedtime story. My kids' favorite bedtime routine was me telling a story: either one from my childhood or a story from the Bible. When I started to include them in the story and began acting out the stories from the Bible, suddenly the interest in my childhood adventures waned. Though they still liked the stories where I got into trouble with Grandma and Grandpa, whose childhood could compare to the adventures and excitement of the stories in the Bible? Without question, their (and my) favorite stories were the stories of Jesus.

The bedtime routine had all started with the story of Zacchaeus, the little guy in the Bible who climbed up a tree to see Jesus because he was too short to see over the crowd. I was feeling rambunctious that night and so to the wide-eyed delight of the girls, I shinnied up the doorframe of the bedroom door and craned my neck to "see Jesus." The girls loved it and were making so much noise my wife, Andrea, came to see about the commotion. There I was clinging to the doorframe like a koala bear with a sheepish look on my face. In response to her incredulous query, I said that I wasn't a koala bear, I was Zacchaeus, and because it was a Bible story technically I *was* putting the girls to bed.

She encouraged me to find some more sedate stories in the Bible to tell, like perhaps Eutychus (the guy in Acts 20 who was "sinking into a deep sleep as Paul talked on and on"). I reminded her that actually that wasn't a very good story since Eutychus was propped up in a window when he fell asleep and ended up falling to his death. (In case you don't know the story, check it out in Acts 20; it has a happy ending.) Come to think of it, my kids would *love* to hear me "tell" that story!

I acted out all kinds of stories from the Bible, but the girls' favorites were stories about Jesus interacting with people, especially the story of Him raising a little girl back to life (Mark 5). Each of my girls—Caylie, Christa, and Julianna—would take turns lying on the bed pretending to be dead (if dead people can giggle), waiting for the moment I would say, in my best Jesus voice, "*Talitha koum!*" which means in Aramaic, "Little girl, I say to you, get up!" They never got tired of that story.

About a year later we moved to another state, and my oldest daughter, Caylie, now nine years old, had her own room. As I was putting her to bed one night she said, "Daddy, can we do a story from the Bible?" and then with hushed excitement added, "I want to be Jesus tonight!" I agreed and we reversed roles. I tried to look as dead as possible, and upon the command to rise I opened my eyes to the most excited face I have ever seen. By the next night, word of this adventurous turn had made it to Christa and

Julianna, and as I walked into the room I was met with a little trio in unison: "Daddy, I want to be Jesus tonight!"

The Hope of the World

Imagine with me for a moment what it would actually be like for us to "be Jesus" to those around us. What if Christians were to live up to our name (Christian means "little Christ") and actually "be Jesus" to our neighbors, those with whom we work, those we see throughout the day? What if, like Jesus, we were to notice the hurting, feel compassion, and reach out a helping hand? What if we loved the Bible like Jesus did when He walked the earth, our daily lives shaped and molded by the Word of God? What if our schoolteachers, our police, and our governmental leaders were all people who loved like Jesus?

Please don't rush too fast past this imaginary exercise. Let's linger for a moment longer. What would happen in our world if more people were more like Jesus? Would it make a difference? Would our world be a better place? Wouldn't the crime rate be lower? Wouldn't the need for police eventually decrease? Wouldn't the need for expensive government agencies that help people be reduced?

What if more people spent less money on entertainment and more on helping people in need? Not one or two people, but thousands, maybe even millions of people. What if one million people ate out one time less each month and used that money to help real people in need? What if? Do you know that America throws away nearly half its food, more than enough to feed the poor of the world? What if we stopped wasting and started giving?

What if more of our world leaders were more like Christ? Imagine the global summits that might be convened to help needier countries instead of fighting over borders and broken treaties.

Does this sound too idealistic? It might if we also imagine that this would happen because of some governmental campaign or altruistic leaders who recognized the moral and ethical value of modeling our lives after the ideal represented in Jesus Christ. We know that will never happen. Becoming like Christ is impossible from mere human effort. Becoming like Christ doesn't come from outside in but from the inside out; it's a matter of our heart and soul.

Jesus gave a crystal clear picture of our hearts when He said: "For from within, out of men's hearts, come evil thoughts, sexual immorality, theft, murder, adultery, greed, malice, deceit, lewdness, envy, slander, arrogance and folly" (Mark 7:21-22). You can't legislate morality; no law or campaign has the power to change a person's heart. But that's just the point: Christianity is not a religious campaign to improve society. *It's a way of living in intimacy with God where our appetite for adventure and beauty is both satisfied and intensified in knowing and loving God.* That love spills out into our relationships with others, and we genuinely love and serve with joy and fulfillment.

Christianity is getting our hearts changed by coming to Christ and then growing to become more like Christ. The by-product is a changed society: changed hearts lead to changed people, which leads to changed society. Bill Hybels, pastor of Willow Creek Community Church near Chicago, has made famous the phrase "the church is the hope of the world." With utmost respect for Bill, I'd like to edit that to say "the *Christlike* church is the hope of the world." When I look at Willow Creek's track record (not merely their often misunderstood reputation) I see a church that is making an impact on the world *because* it is taking seriously the biblical concept of discipleship, reaching people far from God and seriously engaging in the long process of helping them to become more like Christ.

We need more leaders and churches that understand the necessity of and strategy for helping people not only come to Christ but to become more like Christ. The world needs for the church to be more like Christ. In fact, the most crucial need in the world today is for the people of God, the church, to be Christlike.

In a scary prophetic fulfillment of Proverbs 29:18, the church today languishes for lack of vision. We have lost the dream of being salt and light in this world. The church is supposed to make an impact on society, and when we live more like Christ we will. Jesus said, "Let your light shine before men, that they may see your good deeds and praise your Father in heaven" (Matthew 5:16). Can you imagine a world where people, many people, are more and more like Christ? Are we so jaded and cynical that we can't imagine this? This is the dream that God dreamed when He created humanity.

God's Plan for the Human Race

The story of creation in Genesis 1 tells us clearly of God's plan for the human race. He says in Genesis 1:26 (NLT), "Let us make human beings in our image, to be like us." Then in verse 27: "So God created human beings in his own image, in the image of God he created them; male and female he created them."

We will talk more about what it means to be made in the image of God later on in the book, but here we want to see God's original design, His Plan A. We were created in the image of God, to be like God in the way we love and think and relate and act. Twenty-nine verses later begins the sad story of The Fall of humanity, a Fall so dramatic it would "knock the breath" out of us. We were created in the image of God to represent Him in our world: to love like God, to relate like God, to fulfill His purposes on the earth. We were created to relate *to* God in intimacy and love with no barriers or hindrances. That kind of loving is ultimate fulfillment; it satisfies and completes us.

But sin changed all that.

When Adam and Eve sinned, they "fell" out of intimate relationship with God and into a life of sin, pain, shame, and death. As the representatives of the human race before God, their sin introduced and unleashed the forces of death and evil into the human heart. The image of God within them was not removed, but it was corrupted, distorted, and severely marred.

Sin separated corrupt humanity from God, who is holy, and destroyed the purity of the relationship. In its place remains the hollow echo, the shadow of the memory of that relationship—a deep and desperate longing for God. But the echo is so distorted, the image so marred, that people don't recognize the longing as a hunger for relationship with God and seek to fill that yearning with substitutes. The history of humanity is the story of each generation inventing substitute activities and experiences to quench the primordial longing for God. Proverbs 14:12 says, "There is a way that seems right to a man, but in the end it leads to death."

We weren't the only ones longing for the restoration of that intended intimate relationship. God created us to be in relationship because He is a relational God. Our sin breaks the heart of God in ways we will never know. He is the ultimate example of spurned love, rejected by our futile attempts to find life and fulfillment somewhere else, anywhere else besides Him. Undaunted, God, who is love, set into motion Plan B, not an afterthought but a plan the Bible says was prepared before the world began. The image of God in humanity needed to be repaired, restored, and redeemed, and there was only one way it could happen. In love, God made a way for us to get back into intimate relationship with Him. John 3:16 captures Plan B best: "God loved the world so much that he gave his one and only Son, so that everyone who believes in him will not perish but have eternal life."

God sent His Son Jesus to show us what it looks like to be in intimate relationship with Him and to make a way for us to be reconciled to God and begin the restoration process in line with His original design. Christ's life is a model and example, and faith in Christ's death and resurrection is the only way back to God. Jesus lived His life in such a way that He put on display what God's original design looked like for humanity. Living in intimate relationship with His heavenly Father, Jesus loved God, loved people, and lived surrendered.

Jesus' earthly life was so attractive and contagious that people came from miles to hear Him, meet Him, and follow Him. The way He treated people, the stories He told, the things He said and did kept people enthralled. The Gospel of Mark captures this magnetism over and over again: "the people were amazed at his teaching" and "many who heard him were amazed" (Mark 1:22, 6:2). His eventual death on the cross not only didn't stop people's fascination with Him, it intensified it.

Almost two thousand years later, Jesus is still without question the most talked about and written about person in history. People from every nation and culture who have heard about Jesus are drawn to Him like a moth to a flame. He has captivated people from all walks of life. His message has reached poor and rich, young and old, educated and uneducated. Historians, philosophers, and scientists (even atheists) have been fascinated by His life and teachings. Millions upon millions throughout history have surrendered their lives to Jesus Christ to follow Him and become His disciples.

Dirty Little Secret

But there's a dirty little secret about following Jesus that few want to talk about: many Christians are discouraged and confused about what it really means to follow Jesus and have settled for something much less than what the Bible actually teaches. There exists a rather sizable disconnect between the message of the Bible and people's real, everyday lives.

Some are aware of this disconnect and continue to wrestle with it; many don't even realize what has happened and have bought into a cultural Christianity that has them blinded and deceived. This is all the more difficult since every generation has to translate the Christian faith into its own culture. Separating the cultural trappings of Christianity from the core message of Christ involves more discernment and difficulty than most realize. The fact is many Christians have had the "breath knocked out of them" and sadly have ceased following Jesus, settling for a lifeless religious routine instead.

Life is difficult and at times can be daunting to those who want to follow Jesus seriously. You may be reading this book because you are one of those who longs for more. You want to become more like Christ, but something happened; you got the wind knocked out of you and now you're gasping for air.

Getting the breath knocked out of you may be a traumatic event or a slow process of getting burned out. Sometimes we have seasons where life just feels like we're trying to sprint full speed in deep, loose sand. Becoming like Christ just feels like one more demand in our already crazy life.

Like Mike and Alissa from chapter one, mere involvement in church doesn't make you more like Christ any more than going to McDonald's makes you a hamburger. We've heard the sermons, read the books, tried the devotionals, and made the commitments, and looking back it feels like nothing's changed. The honest truth is that for many people life has become a grind, a treadmill, the survival of the fittest. We're back wondering if those typical responses of chapter one aren't accurate after all:

- Christlikeness is a pipedream
- Christlikeness is an arrogant aspiration
- Christlikeness is just for the spiritual superstars

Good, sincere Christians ask, "Where is this abundant life? Is this all there is?"

What if there was a way of living that rises above mere survival, a life of purpose and significance, a life like Christ? There is. There is a way of living like Christ, and the biggest clue is right under your nose: we just need to learn to breathe. God has created a way for you to become like Christ that is as ancient as the Garden of Eden but as relevant as the last breath you just took a second ago. We need to learn to breathe spiritually the way we breathe physically.

Everyone already knows how to do the most important *action* in life; we need to learn how to apply it to the most important *area* of life. That's what the next chapters are all about. And in order to explain what I mean, I need to introduce you to someone. Someone you absolutely must meet. Your life depends on it.

. . . .

CHAPTER THREE

Spiritual Oxygen

I n one sense, the person I want to introduce you to in this chapter needs no introduction. He is one of the featured characters in the most popular, bestselling book in the history of the world (the Bible.) And yet on the other hand He definitely needs an introduction because He's so quiet (even shy) He will never introduce Himself. He needs an introduction precisely because He is so important yet misunderstood. Some people purposely ignore Him, forget about Him, or refer to Him as an "it," while others are afraid of Him, blame Him, or credit Him with some of the craziest things you've ever heard of happening in church.

Since He is so misunderstood, let's go to the person who knows Him best: Jesus. It's always better to hear an introduction from those who know someone well. The person I want to introduce to you is the third person of the Trinity . . . drum roll, please . . . the Holy Spirit.

A Famous Introduction

You might be surprised to find out when and where Jesus introduces the Holy Spirit; it's at a famous meal Jesus is having with His disciples called the Last Supper. The disciples didn't know it was the Last Supper. For them it was special because it was the annual Passover meal, the meal that commemorated the ancient Israelites' exodus out of Egypt, and they were eating it with their rabbi and friend, Jesus. But after Jesus died, was resurrected, and ascended into heaven, the disciples realized how significant it was and later dubbed it the Last Supper and then eventually the Lord's Supper. The evening begins in John 13 and contains some of the most important teaching Jesus ever gave.

John's Gospel, which has more teaching on the Holy Spirit than any other book, actually only records Jesus using the name "Holy Spirit" two times throughout the whole book and only once here where He introduces Him. I have to admit when I discovered this truth it surprised me. Of course, He uses the word "Spirit" more than that but only uses His name, "Holy Spirit," once here and once after His resurrection near the end of the book. Jesus will not only introduce Him, He takes the time to tell His disciples all about Him before the actual introduction. It's recorded for us in John 14-17. Of all times, it's the last night Jesus has with the disciples before He gets arrested, falsely tried, beaten, and crucified on the cross. Why here? Why now?

It was a confusing night for the disciples, a dinner they would never forget. Jesus was saying a lot of things they didn't understand, and fear was sneaking into their hearts. Jesus was talking about leaving them and going to a place where He said they couldn't follow; that was upsetting enough. Then Jesus said that one of them would betray Him and the rest of them would deny Him. They reacted with fear, panic, confusion, troubled hearts, and lots of questions.

The Gift of the Holy Spirit

It was in this troubling context of fear and confusion that Jesus chose to teach His disciples for the first time about the Holy Spirit. <u>Often fear has to do with the anticipation</u> <u>of loss of some kind: loss of control, loss of power, loss</u> <u>of opportunity</u>, etc. It certainly is the case here. But the question remains: why? Why did Jesus pick this time to introduce the Holy Spirit and talk about Him in such detail? Let's dig a little deeper.

John 14:25-27: paraklétos hagios pneuma
                        g3875   g40   g4151

> All this I have spoken while still with you. But the
> <u>Counselor</u>, the <u>Holy Spirit</u>, whom the Father will
> send in my name, will teach you all things and will
> remind you of everything I have said to you. Peace
> I leave with you; my peace I give you. I do not give
> to you as the world gives. Do not let your hearts be
> troubled and do not be afraid.

Jesus chooses this time to introduce the Holy Spirit because it's time to pass the baton. This is a historic night for several reasons, one of them being it is a <u>night of transition</u>. Everything, and I mean everything, will change from this night on. After Jesus' death, the disciples and for that matter the world would never be the same. Jesus knew His disciples were headed into vicious whitewater rapids that would test them like nothing they had ever experienced before. They would need <u>help</u>, <u>counsel</u>, <u>encouragement</u>, <u>reminders</u>, <u>presence, strength</u>—all the very things the Holy Spirit was sent to give. You and I have the same needs, and the Holy Spirit is God's gift to meet those needs and more.

Did you notice the opening words in verse 25, "all this I have spoken"? The "all this" is the teaching that started in John 13. The five chapters of John 13-17 were comprised of dinner conversation, or more accurately dinner teaching. Jesus was pouring out His heart and soul, wrapping up loose ends, preparing His disciples for His death, giving final teaching, and setting the stage for the most dramatic three days in the history of the world. These chapters are full of intensive teaching, profound and concentrated doses of powerful, significant information. And it's just too much for the disciples. Too much data, too much teaching, too much emotion, too much news; they are overwhelmed. So Jesus says, "That's all right. I have told you all this tonight while I am still here, but don't think you have to grasp it all right now. I have a replacement teacher, a counselor who will take it from here. He'll review everything I've said. He will teach you everything you need to know, and even better, He will be with you through all that is to come."

When Jesus referred to this "replacement teacher and counselor" as the "Holy Spirit" and began to introduce who the Holy Spirit was, the disciples were confused. When we put ourselves in their place, we will see it's not as clear whom Jesus was talking about as we might have thought.

The few times in John where Jesus mentioned the Spirit, He was either not with the disciples but with someone else (private meeting with Nicodemus in John 3 and the Samaritan woman at the well in John 4) or He spoke of Him very cryptically, never using His name, Holy Spirit, until here in John 14:26. Then when He does talk about Him in depth in these chapters, Jesus refers to Him with *several* names. He calls Him "Counselor" four times, "Spirit of Truth" three times, and "Holy Spirit" only once! So who is He, this mystical person with multiple names?

Stop

Who is the Holy Spirit?

By far, the most confusing part of the disciples' first hearing about the Holy Spirit was due to the original languages spoken at that time. The disciples heard something different in the phrase "Holy Spirit" than what you're "hearing" or thinking right now. How do I know that? Well, because Jesus was either speaking in Greek or Aramaic (which is a nuance of the Hebrew language), and when He said the word for "spirit," that same word could also mean wind, breath, and air. As you can see from what you just read, in English we have four different words for these realities: spirit, wind, breath, and air. In Hebrew and Aramaic as well as in Greek, they used one word to communicate all four. In Hebrew and Aramaic it's *ruach*. (It's kind of a fun word to say. You've got to get the "ahck" down deep in your throat to get it right.)

Since one word covers four different things, how do you know what a person is talking about when he uses the word *ruach*? Is he talking about wind, is he talking about breath, is he talking about air, or is he talking about the spirit, your spirit, or the Holy Spirit? How do you know? The same thing is true with the Greek word *pneuma* (pronounced nooma). We get our word pneumatic from this word, which refers to pressurized air running through a pipe or hose (like pneumatic tools). *Pneuma* is used for wind, breath, air, and spirit.

Obviously, these four words are extremely similar. It's not like the same word means four completely different things (e.g. tree, taco, hatchet, and donkey). But there's such similarity between wind, breath, air, and spirit that it is difficult to know exactly what the one who spoke meant when he used *pnuema* or *ruach* and what those who heard that same word thought. How are you supposed to know? They had no way of indicating a proper noun through capitalization like we do in English. Of course, context gives us clues most of the time, helping us figure out what the speaker means. But sometimes it's still not clear. This is one of those times.

Scholars argue about which language Jesus spoke most, but my guess is that here, in the intimate setting of the most famous Jewish feast, the Passover, Jesus is speaking Aramaic. It's entirely possible that when Jesus spoke this phrase for the very first time in John 14:26, when He said to them *ruach ha-kodesh* (*kodesh* means "holy"), when He said "holy spirit" in Aramaic, they may have thought "holy wind" or "holy air" or "holy breath." They didn't hear the word "Spirit" conclusively like we do, especially not capitalized. They heard the word *ruach* but may have thought any number of four different words. So it's not immediately obvious who Jesus is talking about. After all, this person Jesus is introducing is invisible, and the Holy Spirit is not a topic that Jesus spent any time talking about up to this point.

For those of you who know your Bibles, you may argue that as good Jews the disciples would have heard of the Holy Spirit because He is mentioned in the Old Testament. He is, but do you know how many times "Holy Spirit" is mentioned in the entire Old Testament? Only twice (Psalm 51:11 and Isaiah 63:10-11)! As a matter of fact, the disciples' familiarity with the Old Testament would have made it even more difficult to know exactly what (actually who) Jesus was referring to. Here's why.

The Old Testament shows such fluidity with this word *ruach*, especially between our concepts of "breath" and "spirit," that they are in many places one and the same. To make matters worse, or better, depending on how you look at it, there are other Hebrew and Aramaic words that get translated "spirit" and "breath" and "wind" interchangeably as well. But don't be dismayed; this actually works to our advantage as we try to uncover exactly whom Jesus meant when He introduced the Holy Spirit.

If your head is spinning right now, don't stop reading. We are about to apply this mini word study to our everyday life in critical, revolutionary ways to help you live the Christian life. When we understand the richness of the Bible's vocabulary and picturesque language, it yields a description of the Holy Spirit that proves extremely valuable and helpful to our lives.

Four Powerful Truths

There are four powerful summary truths about the Holy Spirit that we learn from studying how the Holy Spirit is described in the Bible. Because these are foundational intrinsic realities, I believe Jesus had each one of these truths about the Holy Spirit in mind when He introduced Him to the disciples, and they apply directly to the disciples' and our lives in exciting ways.

The first time the Spirit is mentioned in the Bible is at the dawn of creation. The Bible opens with a picture of the "Spirit of God" mysteriously "hovering over the waters" of a yet unformed earth (Genesis 1:2). The image is of a mist or breath like when you exhale heavily on an icy cold morning.

The very next verse has this Breath/Spirit of God speaking into existence the heavens and the earth, the sun and stars, etc. Psalm 33:6 helps us see how this works: "By the word of the Lord were the heavens made, their starry host by the *breath of his mouth*" (italics added). Both the word for "Spirit" in Genesis 1:2 and the word for "breath" in Psalm 33:6 are the same word, *ruach,* and both scriptures are describing the same creative moment when the Spirit of God spoke the world into existence. The Breath/Spirit of God speaks the Word of God, and the sun and moons and stars leap into existence. That's pretty powerful breath!

Before we move on, I should briefly point out these verses are the beginning of the doctrine of the Inspiration of Scripture. The inspired (in-Spirited) Word of God is "breathed" by God. 2 Timothy 3:16 says it best: "All Scripture is *God-breathed* and is useful for teaching, rebuking, correcting and training in righteousness" (italics added). The Spirit of God breathes the spoken Word of God and the Spirit of God breathes the written Word of God. We will talk much more about this later, but already we can begin to see our first truth about the Holy Spirit: the Holy Spirit is the Breath of God.

Now let's see how this applies directly to our lives. As you know, God didn't stop with just creating the heavens and earth. One of the most fascinating verses in the Bible is Genesis 2:7, which I quoted in chapter one: "the Lord God formed the man from the dust of the ground and breathed into his nostrils the *breath of life*, and the man became a living being" (italics added). The last phrase "living being" could be translated "living breather." The Spirit of God breathes into Adam the breath of life and now Adam lives *as he breathes*. So the first truth about the Holy Spirit is:

1. The Holy Spirit is the Breath of God giving us life

God's Breath, God's Spirit in us, makes us alive. Job 33:4 says, "The Spirit of God has made me; the breath of the Almighty gives me life." The Holy Spirit is like Spiritual Oxygen, holy oxygen. So when Jesus introduces the Holy Spirit, He is beginning to speak about a whole new way of living. God has created us to live inspired (in-Spirited) by His Holy Spirit. The breath we breathe to keep our bodies alive is a powerful picture God designed to show us how to keep our spiritual life alive. We breathe in the Holy Breath (Spirit) of God and He makes our spirit alive. We're back to one of the central phrases of this book: the only way to live is to breathe. Let me put it this way: *the only way to live the Christian life is to breathe the Holy Spirit.* The Holy Spirit is Spiritual Oxygen.

When God made the first man, God didn't breathe for Adam, He breathed into him, but then Adam had to keep breathing. As we will see later on, living in the power of the Spirit is learning how to breathe the Holy Spirit into our lives, how to move in the rhythm and flow of the Holy Spirit in our lives. The Spirit gives, breathes into us, life. The life the Spirit gives is called Spirit-ual life, and the Spiritual life cannot be lived apart from the power and in-breathing of the Holy Spirit. Jesus lived His remarkable life in the power of the Spirit, and as He prepares His disciples for life apart from His physical daily presence, He wants them to know the presence and power of God will be with them.

Breath has a sense of presence to it. When you get close enough to a person to feel (or smell) his breath, there's a sense of immediacy or presence about him. Of course this can be good or bad depending on how comfortable we are being in an intimate space with that person (and what his breath smells like!). When we sense the presence of God, we are sensing the presence of the Holy Breath/Spirit of God. God makes His presence known by the presence and power of the Holy Spirit. The Holy Spirit makes God's presence manifest.

Back to the creation story, we saw the incredible power present in the Breath of God. When He speaks, worlds snap into existence. We call this creation *ex nihilo*: creation out of nothing. God didn't take existing matter and manufacture the sun and stars, the earth and moon. He merely spoke, and where there previously had been nothing, suddenly there were galaxies, planets, peacocks, and giraffes. That's power! With the presence of God comes the power of God.

Incredibly, this power is available to us in the person of the Holy Spirit. This is the second truth we learn about the Holy Spirit:

Stop

2. The Holy Spirit is the Presence of God giving us power

When God breathed into Adam the breath of life, that life was power—power to get up, to walk, to move, to speak. In the same way, when the Spirit of God breathes into our lives as Christians, He gives us the power to live the Christian life, the Christlike life. Without the presence and power of God, we are dead, powerless, unable to live like Christ. In fact, because of our sin, we can't even take a step toward Christ without the power of the Holy Spirit. Jesus said of the Spirit, "When he comes, he will convict the world of guilt in regard to sin and righteousness and judgment" (John 16:8).

The Spirit of God is the one who convicts us of our sin and our need for Jesus as our Savior. This convicting power is a part of the first work of the Holy Spirit in our life. He convicts us of our sin, reveals to us our need for a Savior, and draws us to Christ. No one else in the world has the power to enter a person's heart and mind and convict him of sin.

But surrendering your heart to Christ is just the beginning of your experience of the power of the Holy Spirit. When you surrender your heart and life to Jesus Christ as your Lord and Savior, the Holy Spirit comes fully into your life and by His power regenerates your heart and mind. Jesus said, "I tell you the truth, no one can enter the kingdom of God unless he is born of water and the Spirit" (John 3:5). Jesus described this powerful work of the Spirit as being "born" all over again; He regenerates your heart and gives you a new start, a new birth. Only the Holy Spirit has the power to change a person's heart. Then He begins the process of making you more and more like Christ.

In the first chapter of Acts, just before He ascended into heaven, Jesus told His disciples to stay in Jerusalem and to wait for the Gift of the Holy Spirit, which He said "you have heard me speak about." That statement refers back to the Last Supper teaching time where Jesus introduced the Holy Spirit in John 14-17. Then He adds, "You will receive power when the Holy Spirit comes upon you" (Acts 1:8). The presence of the Holy Spirit brings the power of the Holy Spirit.

Jesus never claimed to rely on His own strength but lived His life in the "power of the Holy Spirit" (Luke 4:14). This point was not lost on Peter as he preached to a group of people in Acts 10 and told "how God anointed Jesus of Nazareth with the Holy Spirit and power, and how he went around doing good and healing all who were under the power of the devil, because God was with him" (Acts 10:38). Not even Jesus lived His life apart from the power of the Holy Spirit. The more you and I learn to cooperate with the Holy Spirit, the more we will see this kind of power in our lives. The Spirit of God *with* us means the power of God is now available *to* us. So the second truth we learn about the Holy Spirit is: the Holy Spirit is the presence of God giving us power.

Let's go back to the night of the Last Supper, the night Jesus introduces the Holy Spirit. The first thing He says about the Spirit that night is rather cryptic and is recorded in John 14:16-17: "I will ask the Father, and he will give you another Counselor to be with you forever—the Spirit of truth . . . you know him, for he lives with you and will be in you." This verse is groundbreaking for understanding the role of the Holy Spirit in our lives, and we will draw our remaining truths from it. Notice the phrases "be *with* you" and "lives *with* you" (italics mine). While there is a lot to learn about who the Spirit is, it seems the first thing Jesus wants them to see that night is that the Holy Spirit would be with them, helping them to live. That is our third truth about the Holy Spirit.

3. The Holy Spirit is God with us helping us to live

When Jesus was born, the Gospel of Matthew (1:23) records that His miraculous birth took place to fulfill what had been prophesied in Isaiah, that Jesus would be called Immanuel, which means "God with us." So when Jesus came to earth and walked among us, He was "God with us," God talking and teaching and healing and loving. But back once more to John 14:25-27, there is a tone of foreboding in Jesus' phrase "all this I have spoken, while I am *still with you*" and "my peace I *leave* with you" (italics added). Jesus is hinting that no longer would God be "with us" as He was in the physical body of Jesus of Nazareth.

It shouldn't take long to feel the disciples' grief, fear, and confusion when Jesus implied that night "I am leaving . . ." and then actually said those very words in John 16:28. Jesus was rocking the disciples' world. But notice what He said just a few verses earlier: "Because I have said these things, you are filled with grief. But I tell you the truth: It is for your good that I am going away. Unless I go away, the Counselor will not come to you; but if I go, I will send him to you."

The disciples are afraid they won't know how to live without Jesus. If Jesus is not with them, they reason, God is not with them. Jesus is trying to help the disciples see that all the wonder and power of sensing the manifest presence of God whenever they were in the physical presence of Jesus would not stop with His death and eventual ascension to heaven in a matter of days.

The presence of God they felt with Jesus would continue to be present with the Holy Spirit. The Spirit would be with them wherever they went. In fact, they would not be able to experience the manifest presence of God no matter where they went *unless* Jesus left. This reality of the Holy Spirit being *with* the disciples wherever they went, helping them live, was the very first thing Jesus said about the Spirit that night. "And I will ask the Father, and he will give you another Counselor to be with you forever—the Spirit of truth."

This promise Jesus makes to the disciples is for you and me as well. The Holy Spirit is God with us, helping us to live. He will be with us forever. He will be our Counselor, our Helper—the One who comes alongside us and helps us through the most difficult circumstances of life. Counselors guide, they help us sort through difficulties, to get perspective. Counselors help us see the truth about ourselves, about God, and about life. The Holy Spirit is the preeminent Counselor, who not only shows us the truth but is Himself the Spirit of Truth.

Before we move away from these verses, let's not overlook something very significant about Jesus' language regarding the Holy Spirit. Did you see the personal pronouns "him" and "he" in the phrase "you know *him* for *he* lives with you"? The Holy Spirit is a life-giving, powerful *Person*, not some mysterious force. To live in the power of the Spirit is not to be connected to some life force but to be connected to God Himself.

Let me just get really clear. The Holy Spirit is not merely the presence of God, the Breath of God. He *is* God. That's why we should never refer to the Holy Spirit as an "it." He is God, the third Person of the Trinity. So Jesus is saying the Holy Spirit is God Himself, living with us, helping us to live as disciples of Christ.

The last words of verse 17 reveal one more powerful truth about the Holy Spirit that Jesus wants the disciples to see: the day is coming when the Holy Spirit "will be in you."

Jesus is saying, "You thought it was cool having Me, 'God with us,' to hang around with; it gets even better. With the coming of the Holy Spirit, no longer will He be 'God with you,' He will be 'God *in* you!'" This is the amazing and life-transforming truth Jesus is referring to: God will fill our lives with the same Holy Spirit that filled Jesus. This is the fourth and culminating truth about the Holy Spirit:

4. The Holy Spirit is God in us making us more like Christ

When Jesus said "he will be in you" He was speaking about a reality that had only been hinted at in the Old Testament, but which was the secret to Jesus' life: the indwelling of the Holy Spirit. This is the most important reality for us to grasp in seeking to become like Christ.

The college I graduated from has as its motto "the Spirit makes the Difference." How true! He makes the difference between life and death, between bearing fruit or stagnating, between empowered Christianity and empty striving. Without the Holy Spirit, we cannot live a Christlike life. But when we learn to practice Spiritual Breathing and live surrendered to the Holy Spirit, He makes the difference in our lives, forming the Christlike life within us.

Years later, the apostle Paul grasped this truth and it revolutionized his life. Apart from Jesus Himself, nobody understood better the significance of God filling us with His Holy Spirit. Paul wrote about his own attempts to live up to God's standards, with every failure only underscoring his inability to live as he knew he should.

Everyone falls short of living as God designed; all our attempts at finding life on our own are futile striving. Paul calls our striving and failing death and says everyone is "dead in their trespasses and sins." Then he shows how Jesus' death and resurrection not only pays the penalty for our sin, it also makes it possible for us to receive a brand-new life from the inside out. The same power that was at work in raising Jesus from the dead (the Holy Spirit) is at work in us empowering us to live the Christian life.

Romans 8:11 (NLT) says, "The Spirit of God, who raised Jesus from the dead, lives in you. And just as God raised Christ Jesus from the dead, he will give life to your mortal bodies by this same Spirit living within you." In this verse,

Paul invites us to picture the dead mortal body of Jesus, a corpse lying in a tomb, with no breath in it. Purposely reminiscent of Adam's lifeless body at creation, Paul describes the Breath/Spirit of God once again breathing life into a man, raising Him to new life.

If Paul succeeded at conveying the incredible role of the Holy Spirit in raising Christ from the dead, then it should leave us with our mouths gaping open to think that this same powerful presence of the Breath/Spirit of God is *in us* giving us new life!

Like Adam in the dust and Jesus in the tomb, we also are powerless to give ourselves new life. We cannot make ourselves alive. But, just as important, we cannot live this new life apart from the life-giving Breath/Spirit of God. No amount of being good or doing good can help us reach the goal of Christlikeness. Only the Spirit breathing the life of Christ in us can help us become more like Christ.

The Process of Christlikeness

Some people picture the process of Christlikeness to be like pushing a heavy object up a hill. It's hard work, but if you do the right things, stay at it, keep pushing, and don't give up, eventually you reach your destination. We think it is through our striving to do the Christlike thing in every situation that we in due course arrive at Christlikeness. This kind of thinking explains why there are so many burned-out Christians, exhausted from trying to be like Christ or just giving up altogether.

Incredulous that Christians would even try such a thing, Paul asks a group of people in the first century: "Are you so foolish? After beginning with the Spirit, are you now trying to attain your goal by human effort?" (Galatians 3:3) Just as in Paul's day, if we were forced to answer this rhetorical question, many would have to answer with a sheepish "yes."

One of the burdens of Paul's life was to help people see the power of the Spirit available to us to make us more like Christ. Listen to the passion and pathos in his voice just a few verses later: "Oh, my dear children! I feel as if I'm going through labor pains for you again, and they will continue until Christ is fully developed in your lives" (Galatians 4:19 NLT).

Mothers who have experienced severe pain in giving birth might be inclined to focus on the "labor pains" part of that verse, but I want to focus on the phrase "until Christ is fully developed in your lives." The NIV and other translations capture a significant Greek word in that phrase when they translate this verse, "until Christ is *formed* in you." The Greek word is *morphoo* (pronounced mor-phóh-oh) and refers to something being formed, shaped, and molded. In ancient Greece, *morphoo* was used to refer to the work of artists to describe how they would fashion their material into a particular image.

When I was in junior high school, our art teacher, Mrs. Hastings, was convinced that all of us had an "inner artist" just waiting to get out. All we needed was the right medium, and this little "inner artist" would come bursting forth. So she ran us through the gauntlet of one art medium after another. We drew, painted (with watercolor, acrylic, by brush, by finger, smeared with our hands, threw paint against walls), sculpted, used paper maché, clay—a seemingly endless barrage of art forms were imposed upon us.

The projects that came out of that art room *really* broadened the definition of art and certainly must have challenged Mrs. Hastings' "inner artist" theory. Undaunted, she taught that course for years, a sterling example of someone carried along by an idealistic theory undeterred by evidence to the contrary.

My mother was going through old boxes in the attic a number of years ago and came across one of my seventh grade art projects in clay. I looked at it for a couple of minutes trying to imagine what this painted glob of dried mud was intended to communicate. It was clear what the look on my face was communicating: bewilderment. After about a minute, it hit me what I must have done: I had just squeezed the clay in my hands and extracted my fingers and thumbs, leaving holes and crevices that matched up perfectly (though a little smaller) with my hands many years later. Surely that project should have shaken Mrs. Hastings' theory. My memory of her though is that of a perpetual first-time mother admiring the art of her three-year-old. Come to think of it, she was perfect for that job.

Thankfully, the Holy Spirit is a much better match with the word artist than I am. In fact, as we saw earlier by admiring His work in creation, the Spirit of God is the ultimate artistic craftsman, and His work in us doesn't stop at creating us. His greatest work is in re-creation, taking sin-infested image-bearers like you and me and restoring and forming us into the image of Jesus Christ.

As Paul tried to describe this miraculous work he often used this word *morphoo* to communicate what God is doing in Christ through the power of the Holy Spirit. Romans 8:29 is one such example. Paul says that God is using everyday life (see the "all things" of v. 28) to make us like Christ, working in us until we are *"conformed* to the likeness of his Son."

"Conformed" translates a different form of the word *morphoo,* which is the word *summorphizo* and means "to form like." It's the word used to shape and form something so that it is like something else. My adventure in clay was bizarrely unique, unlike anything else. But God is shaping us to be like Christ, and the *something* that He is shaping is our character.

When God designed you in your mother's womb He gave you unique physical DNA that determined your hair and eye color, your personality, etc. Every single person is unique, "fearfully and wonderfully made." Those attributes are part of what make you *you*; God doesn't want to change that, He made you that way!

The Character of Christ

What God is changing and forming and shaping is our heart and our character so that we have the character of Christ. God wants us to love like Christ, to forgive like Christ, to be generous like Christ, to reach out with compassion like Christ. The "all things" in verse 28 that He is using is everything in our lives: difficult times, exciting times, mundane times, adversity, prosperity, joy, sadness, love, disappointment, trials, etc.

The Spirit of God uses the truth of God's Word and ordinary life to form Christlikeness in us. Most people recognize that God is working in them when they hear a sermon or read the Bible or pray. But few recognize that God is always at work, and He wants to use every circumstance of our lives to make us more like Christ. We tend to think of spiritual growth happening at special moments or spiritual moments. But every moment is a spiritual moment once we learn how to cooperate with the Holy Spirit.

My favorite form of this word *morphoo* shows up just four chapters later in the Book of Romans. Romans 12:2 says, "Do not conform any longer to the pattern of this world, but be *transformed* by the renewing of your mind" (italics added). The word for transform is *metamorphoo* which means to "transform the essential nature of." The Holy Spirit is conforming us to be more like Christ as He "transforms our essential nature." Because of sin, our essential nature has been distorted and is self-centered and self-focused.

The work of the Holy Spirit in us transforms that essential self-centeredness into Christlikeness. It's a lifelong process that is pictured for us in the last time this word shows up in the Bible, 2 Corinthians 3:18, where Paul says through the work of the Holy Spirit we "are being *transformed* into his likeness." The NLT puts it this way: "And the Lord—who is the Spirit—makes us more and more like him as we are changed into his glorious image."

Just as a highly skilled artist shapes and forms his artistic masterpiece until it conforms to the image he has in his mind, so the Holy Spirit is working in us to make us more like Christ. This forming process happens from the inside out; it's not outside-in striving, but inside-out transformation. Because the Spirit works in our heart, He is breathing His life-giving and transforming creative power into that very place that shapes our desires, our will, our hopes, our goals. We find ourselves wanting to be more loving, more compassionate, more generous. We find ourselves hungering for the Word of God, desiring to love God and love people just like Christ.

Several years ago my family and I were visiting a park developed around a fort built in the 1700s where they had recreated the living and working conditions of early American history. As we walked through the fort, viewing the candle-makers, blacksmiths, and cobblers, I was especially drawn to the glassblowers. I stood there entranced as they heated the sand, soda, and lime to extremely hot temperatures and then began the simple but highly skilled process of glassblowing, creating one-of-a-kind glass bowls, bottles, cups, and ornaments.

I was amazed at how these glassblowers would work with just a blob of glass right out of the fire, insert a blowpipe into it, and then with mostly the breath of their lungs and the tipping and angle of the glass create masterpieces. Each one was unique, formed one at a time by the skilled "breathing into" of these artists.

Far beyond the creativity of a glassblower is the work of the Holy Spirit as He breathes into us His breath of life, forming and shaping us as He breathes and tips and angles, lovingly and expertly crafting spiritual masterpieces. His work gives the triune God great joy, Father, Son, and Holy Spirit rejoicing over the transformation of our lives to become more like Christ.

This is why Ephesians 5:18 says "keep on being filled with the Spirit"; we need to learn how to breathe God's Spiritual Oxygen. The only way to live is to breathe. We want to learn how to live "filled with the Spirit" so we are alive and vibrant spiritually. We want to live "filled with the Spirit" so the Holy Spirit has something to work with to help us become like Christ.

We began this chapter at the dinner table with Jesus and His disciples as Jesus introduced the Holy Spirit. We saw that He is the One who is:

1. The Breath of God giving us life
2. The Presence of God giving us power
3. God with us helping us to live
4. God in us making us more like Christ

I asked you to think with me about why Jesus chose this night—this night of the Lord's Supper, this night when He's going to turn to His disciples and say "this bread is My body given for you; this cup is My blood shed for you." Why this night to introduce the Holy Spirit? The symbolism of the Lord's Supper is a powerful and beautiful picture of what God has done for us on the cross. But there may be even more symbolic truth here than we have ever seen before.

The Power of the Blood

One of Jesus' favorite teaching methods was to impart spiritual realities through natural and physical examples. The physical and natural world is a reflection of the spiritual world. The physical body and blood of Jesus would be a symbol of the spiritual reality of the sacrificial death of Jesus for the forgiveness of sins. Hebrews 9:22 says that "without the shedding of blood, there can be no forgiveness of sins."

The Bible teaches that when Jesus died on the cross, His blood, the blood of the sinless Son of God, paid the penalty for your sin and mine; that His blood washes away our sin, forgives us, and makes us right with God. This is the power of the blood to wash away our sin. If you're a Christian today, it's because the blood of Jesus Christ was shed for you and by faith you understood and accepted this and surrendered your life to Christ as your Savior and Lord.

But why blood? Ever wonder that?

Scientists have discovered fascinating information about blood that reflects even more astounding truths about God's choice of blood as "the forgiving agent." Blood is a mixture of plasma (which is 90 percent water) and cells that float in the plasma. Red blood cells are the most numerous, making up 40-45 percent of one's blood, and they carry what you might say makes the blood alive: oxygen. Without oxygen, the blood is unable to deliver "life" to the body. When Leviticus 17:14 says "the life is in the blood," it is true spiritually, physically, and medically. How does oxygen get into the blood?

When I breathe, I inhale the oxygen in the air through my mouth or nose, and then it goes down my trachea or windpipe (the breathing tube) into the lungs. There are hundreds of thousands of little bronchial branches that spread out into our lungs, and at the end of these bronchial tubes are little air sacs called alveoli. (I know, sounds like ravioli.) Each lung has 150-250 million alveoli, and they are the transfer systems that assimilate the oxygen into the blood.

God has designed your body so that it breathes in the oxygen in the air, and transfers it to the blood, which then cleanses and nourishes and keeps your body alive. The oxygen- rich blood brings life and healing to our body; it purifies our body. If there's no oxygen in blood, blood is of no value. But if you infuse blood with oxygen, then truly, "the life is in the blood."

So here's the picture: the night that Jesus introduces the Lord's Supper, the night He proclaims His blood for the forgiveness of sins, is the *very same night* He introduces the Holy Spirit, the Breath of God—the Spiritual Oxygen of God! Is that a coincidence? I don't think so. The Holy Spirit is Spiritual Oxygen; He is the One who gives life to the blood! He applies the blood of Jesus Christ to my soul, cleansing me, forgiving me, making me a new person. Hallelujah! It is the Holy Spirit, the Breath of God, infused into the blood of Jesus, that makes salvation applicable to my life. The Spirit and the blood give witness that the blood of Christ and the Breath of God come together and make your salvation a reality.

We must not separate the cross of Christ from the resurrection of Christ, and we must not separate those two realities from the coming of the Holy Spirit. Jesus' death, His resurrection, and the coming of the Spirit all come together to make real our new life in Christ. And that's why the very night of Jesus' resurrection from the dead, the most incredible day in history, was capped off with Jesus appearing to His disciples, recorded for us in John 20:22: "And Jesus breathed on them and said receive the Holy Spirit."

Look how Jesus brings all this together. He is saying, "My Breath, as the Second Person of the Trinity, my Breath is the Holy Breath of God. I'm breathing out Spiritual Oxygen, I'm breathing out the life of God, the power of God, and I'm breathing on you, My disciples. Receive the Holy Spirit." And it's a taste of what's to come just fifty days later when the Holy Spirit descends on the disciples and empowers and enlivens them to begin to live lives of Christlikeness. Indeed, "the Spirit makes the Difference!"

· ·

CHAPTER FOUR

Introducing Christlikeness

I remember the summer pop music icon Michael Jackson died. His death set off a media frenzy dominating the news with stories of his life and rise to stardom as the "King of Pop." There seemed to be a special fascination in comparing his life and death to that of Elvis Presley, the so-called "King of Rock" who died in 1977. Many of the articles and documentaries noted how people not only admired these music legends, they *wanted to be like them.*

If you wanted to "be like Christ," where would you start?

For days after Jackson's death, fans dressed up like him gathered around his star on Hollywood Boulevard and in front of his mansion. People tried to imitate his dancing style, his wardrobe, and his singing voice. In Elvis' case, over thirty years after his death, there are still numerous Elvis impersonators in nightclubs and talent contests.

The Bible speaks of "imitating Christ." If I want to imitate Christ, does that mean I dress up in a bathrobe and sandals? Grow a beard and learn Aramaic? Walk around speaking in parables and drawing in the sand?

Crowds at athletic events are filled with young and old alike wearing the jersey and number of their favorite star player. When I was younger, the chant was to "be like Mike" referring to basketball legend Michael Jordan. Everyone is clear on what it means to "be like Mike," but what does it mean to "be like Christ"? What part of Christ's life would one seek to emulate?

A popular book in America for many years was Charles Sheldon's *In His Steps* where these questions of Christlikeness were tackled via a novel. Sheldon depicted characters asking the now famous question "What Would Jesus Do?" as they faced significant moments of crisis, temptation, or need in their life.

Dallas Willard, the latest sage in the history of spiritual formation, in his book *The Spirit of the Disciplines*, showed the folly of seeking to do what Jesus did during crisis moments without practicing what Jesus did in the normal course of our life. If we don't practice living a life as Jesus did in the mundane moments of life, we won't be able to "do what Jesus did" in the crises. It becomes another version of striving to be like Christ in our own strength, just with the added help of the memorable little acronym WWJD to prompt us to do the Christlike thing.

Instead, becoming like Christ is living each day as Jesus would if He were living in our body. We align our lives around certain practices and disciplines modeled in the life of Christ and developed throughout Christian history, and over time we begin to live more and more like Christ.

John Ortberg, deeply influenced by Willard, pictures it as the difference between *trying* to be like Christ and *training* to be like Christ. His illustration is the marathon. While very few of us could run a marathon today, no matter how hard we tried, almost all of us could do it within a year or so if we trained properly. What is impossible to do by merely trying harder becomes possible through proper training. The training and disciplines produce the desired product.

A Dangerous Assumption

Willard's language is a helpful corrective to the viewpoint prevalent in some circles that takes what I call the "assumptive approach" to Christian maturity. The "assumptive approach" assumes that Christian spiritual formation is automatic and inevitable as we walk through life. The Holy Spirit is seen as the One who mysteriously and inexorably works to grow us into spiritual maturity, plodding along a predestined route toward an inevitable goal that we unwittingly assent to.

An analogy might be getting into the current of a river moving toward the ocean. Our lives are like canoes carried along by the current of the river of the Spirit; it might help if we paddled, but it's not critical since, because of the current, we'll get there eventually. Your effort doesn't really matter, it's impossible to paddle upstream, and eventually the irresistible grace of God overcomes your inadequacies and struggles and carries you to the inevitable destination. This seems to make sense to many Christians largely because we recognize the futility of rowing upstream and many of us understand that we don't become like Christ through striving and depending on human effort. But *depending on* effort is not corrected by *expending no* effort.

Proponents of this "assumptive approach" cite the parallel between our physical bodies and our spiritual life. The reasoning goes like this: kids automatically grow up physically and the same must be true spiritually. There is actually some truth to this line of thinking. The only problem is that we don't pay attention to the necessary growth requirements nearly as closely in our spiritual lives as we do for our physical bodies. Bodies don't automatically grow. They only grow when you surround them with oxygen, feed them with proper nourishment, provide them with ample water, and exercise and rest them regularly.

We understand that our physical bodies need oxygen, food, water, rest, and exercise, but do we know what that looks like spiritually? Many people from this school of thought equate going to church and reading the Bible with spiritual nutrition. But merely going to church and reading the Bible doesn't nourish you any more than watching the Food Network on cable TV. Watching other people cook and eat is not the same thing as eating and digesting the food into your own body. Too many people still unwittingly buy into thinking that information equals transformation. Hearing information and even being able to recite it back is not the same thing as digesting the Word of God into our lives and applying it to our lives, letting it change the way we act and interact with God and other people.

Both of these philosophies (the biblical "training for Christlikeness" and the dangerous "assuming automatic growth") are better than the heretical idea of trying to earn my salvation and work my way to spiritual maturity on my own, but I believe there may still be some sticking points in how we apply the best teaching on becoming like Christ to our lives. Though I align myself closely with the "Willard School of Spiritual Formation" (training for Christlikeness), I wonder if in our attempts to apply his teaching, too many of us have put too much emphasis on disciplines and virtues and not enough on more actively and dynamically cooperating with the primary work of the Spirit. It seems we have only applied part of Willard's excellent teaching on becoming like Christ.

Willard adamantly opposes seeking to become like Christ apart from the Spirit (as he should, since it is impossible), and, especially in his book *Renovation of the Heart*, underlines the necessity for us to cooperate with the Spirit as we grow as disciples. Furthermore, his school of thought maintains that the spiritual disciplines are *how* we cooperate with the Spirit's work. I agree, but in my work with people it seems folks need more, perhaps even more basic, help knowing how to cooperate with the Spirit. Instead of moving away from Willard's approach, I want to extend it into more application. I seek to contribute to his call for a "curriculum of Christlikeness."

In addition, I wonder if there's a way of taking "dependence on the Spirit" and adding to it a more intentional recognition of what the Spirit is doing and then more deliberately aligning and cooperating with Him.

Too many people fall into one ditch or the other: doing nothing, or working and striving (and sometimes calling it practicing the spiritual disciplines), hoping the Spirit is using our efforts to somehow make us more like Christ. I meet a lot of discouraged Christians who have either bailed or burned out on discipleship. I wonder if there is a way to more closely align ourselves with what Christ did and what the Spirit is doing.

A New Look at the Life of Christ

To that end, I did a thorough re-examination of the life of Christ in the Gospels seeking two things:

- a fresh summary of the core characteristics of Christ's life; and,
- how Jesus cooperated with the work of the Holy Spirit

As I embarked on this study, I believed the interface of these two dynamics (characteristics of Christ and cooperating with the Spirit) would give us some serious traction in our attempts to become more like Christ.

The discoveries I made were nothing less than life-changing. Things I had studied for years suddenly came into focus; disparate pieces of truth came into alignment. It was like "Aha!" stuck on repeat mode. Even more exciting was seeing the impact on others. I wrote three seminars to pass along my discoveries, each one full of teaching, exercises, insights, and skill development. I was stunned at the responses and comments people made as they took each seminar.

One of the motivations for writing this book has been the repeated requests and encouragements from people to put this into book form. There is nothing new here; in fact, the whole point has been to try to recapture the central characteristics in the life of Christ while He walked and talked and lived His remarkable life on this earth.

Some of my language will resemble that of classic spiritual disciplines, while in other places I seek to show how classic spiritual disciplines (e.g. humility) come as a surprising *result* of a shift in orientation, attitudes, and actions. Instead of focusing on the discipline and virtue, I believe a different approach yields a more Christlike result. All the best writers on the spiritual disciplines argue that the focus should never be on the discipline anyway, but some of their approaches seem to make that a practical impossibility.

As Dallas Willard repeatedly reminded us, our focus is clear and certain: Jesus Christ. The goal is to know Him, love Him, trust Him, and become more like Him. As we will see, we want to follow Jesus, learn from Jesus, and become more like Jesus. A careful and thorough re-examination of the Gospels is the best place to start in seeking to follow Jesus. Seeing His life, hearing His words, watching how He interacted, noting His pattern of life, feeling His heart, and wrestling with His stories are essential and irreplaceable activities in the journey of Christlikeness.

The Secret to Jesus' Life

All along the way, we will be listening and watching for clues as to how Jesus viewed, depended on, and breathed in Spiritual Oxygen, the very Breath of God, known as the Holy Spirit. If there was a secret to Jesus' extraordinary life on earth it was this: *the only way to live is to breathe.* He knew the only way to live as an accurate reflection of the image of God on earth was to breathe in Spiritual Oxygen, the Holy Spirit. He made it abundantly clear that He never sought to do His own thing, say His own words, or go His own way. Jesus lived surrendered to the power of the Holy Spirit, and it made all the difference in the world.

Living dependent on the Spirit must never be construed, however, to mean will-less or aimless, capriciously wandering around with no direction or pattern of life. After all, Jesus did say to His disciples "follow Me" and "learn from Me." And likewise, He left His disciples with the clear mandate known as the Great Commission, to make more disciples. A disciple is one who is becoming like their master. Our Master is Jesus Christ, so Christlikeness is our goal. Luke 6:40 says that when a disciple is "fully trained, he is like his teacher."

Real disciples are people who increasingly live like Jesus Christ. As we cooperate with the Holy Spirit's work in our lives, God will use all of life to help make us like Christ (Romans 8:28-29). The fruit of the Spirit will mature in our lives, we will increasingly reflect Christ in our lives, and God will be glorified in us.

More and more studies are revealing that many Christians have stalled in their faith and have no idea how to get growing again. God wants to catalyze growth in us and help us take our next step in becoming more like Christ.

So what does it look like when we are "like Christ"?

Following Jesus

As we saw, when Jesus called the disciples He said "follow Me." He was inviting them to pattern their lives after the way He lived His. If you study the life of Christ while He was on earth with this simple idea of "following Jesus," you begin to see that His approach to life, how He spent His time, and His actions all came out of a way of viewing God and people that set Him apart from everyone else. His orientation to life produced a manner of living that contains the defining characteristics that He modeled and taught to His disciples. I'm not talking about things like walking on water and stilling storms; I'm talking about the way He lived with God and people, the way He lived His everyday life. This is Christlikeness that is clear and practical, not abstract and ethereal—a way of living that, empowered by the Holy Spirit, is actually doable.

Of course, clear and practical doesn't mean rigid and formulaic. The Bible rejects a cookie-cutter recipe of spiritual formation. Each of us is unique, and God customizes His work in our lives in ways that fit our maturity level, personality, stage in life, upbringing, and learning style. Nobody knows us better than God, and He is working in each of us His customized, dynamic plan to make us like Christ. He sent Jesus to earth not only to die for our sins but to give us a model of how to live, and He gives His Holy Spirit to make that life possible.

I believe Jesus meant it when He said "follow Me," and I believe too many of us have fallen into the extremes of a discipleship that is either watered down into vague moralism, bound up in rigid legalism, or caught up in mystical abstraction. We must restore Christlikeness to a biblical, practical, understandable way of living. While Jesus said and did many things, I believe you can summarize this practical Christlikeness under six distinctives that I call the Core Characteristics of Christlikeness. These Core Characteristics are what we want to explore, understand, and live out in our daily lives. They are what the Holy Spirit is working to produce in our lives through His own curriculum of Christlikeness.

Core Characteristics of Christlikeness

1. Jesus lived connected to God through the Word and prayer.
2. Jesus displayed a heart of worship.
3. Jesus treated all people with grace-filled, other-centered love.
4. Jesus intentionally sought out people to show and share the Good News.
5. Jesus was a Spirit-led, Spirit-empowered servant.
6. Jesus was a trustworthy steward of all God entrusted to Him.

Jesus lived connected to God through the Word and prayer.

Jesus had a remarkable, vibrant connection with the Father that was so vital and central to His life that it literally energized and invigorated Him. We call this connection

Spiritual Breathing. Spiritual Breathing brings the life of the Spirit into our lives. This relationship is sustained and cultivated through absorbing the Word of God into your life and interacting with God through the Word and a life of prayer where you come to know God deeply and develop a foundational dependence on Him. All the other characteristics of Christlikeness are formed from this connection. To be Christlike is to be connected in a growing relationship with God through Spiritual Breathing.

Jesus displayed a heart of worship.

Jesus' life was a life of worship to the Father, led by and filled with the Holy Spirit. He worshipped in Spirit and in truth and said the Father is looking for us to worship in the same way. Worship is an act of Spiritual Breathing, the loving response to God for who He is and what He has done. It is the loving God with all your heart, soul, mind, and strength that Jesus talked about in the Great Commandment (Mark 12:30). Having a heart of worship is cultivating a lifestyle of worship that is all encompassing so that "whatever you do, do it all to the glory of God" (1 Corinthians 10:31). It includes gathering weekly with the local church to express this worship and finding ways throughout the week to express your love for God. To be Christlike is to have a heart of worship.

Jesus related with grace-filled, other-centered love.

Jesus' way of relating to others was revolutionary. The intimate love He experienced in the Trinity spilled out into His sacrificial love for people, epitomized in the cross. Ephesians 5:2 says we are to practice loving "just as Christ loved us and gave himself up for us." To be Christlike is to relate to others with giving, other-centered, and sacrificial love, and this kind of love is distinctly the fruit of cooperating with the Holy Spirit in our lives as we practice Spiritual Breathing.

Jesus intentionally sought out people to show and share the Good News.

Jesus' love for all people, no matter what their economic standing, racial or religious background, no matter their current lifestyle, motivated Him to reach out to them. Jesus came to seek and save the lost (Luke 19:10). He intentionally and consistently lived a life of reaching out in love to others. This is the second part of the Great Commandment in Mark 12:30-31 where we reach out in love to our "neighbors": those "near us" where we live, work, and interact. To be Christlike is to intentionally build redemptive relationships with those outside the kingdom of God, loving them, seeking to meet their practical needs, and sharing with them the Good News of God's love. But it is not merely reaching out and moving on; it is then helping them grow into disciples. It is investing your life in others, building redemptive, reproductive relationships with those outside the kingdom of God to help them come to and then become like Christ. To be Christlike includes helping to reproduce the Christlike life in others. Evangelism, like all ministry, is only effective when it is done in cooperation with the Holy Spirit as we practice Spiritual Breathing.

Jesus was a Spirit-led, Spirit-empowered servant.

Jesus lived His remarkable life in the power of the Holy Spirit. He was led by the Spirit, and He moved in the dynamic flow of the Holy Spirit. He announced that the Spirit of God had anointed Him to serve and love others and then embarked on a life of servanthood in the power of the Spirit. As Christ, He evidenced all the gifts of the Spirit in Himself. As His followers, each of us has been given gifts of the Spirit to use to serve others, build up the body of Christ, and glorify God. To be Christlike is to practice Spiritual Breathing as we listen to the promptings of the Holy Spirit, move in the power of the Spirit, and utilize the gifts of the Spirit to serve others.

Jesus was a trustworthy steward of all God entrusted to Him.

Jesus understood that all we have on earth has been given and entrusted to us by God the Father. Our bodies, our hearts, our minds, our time, our money, our family all belong to Him. He has placed us as stewards of that which He owns and as such will hold us accountable for how we manage His resources. Jesus lived in trusting dependence on the Father through the practice of Spiritual Breathing. Living in dependence on God, He did not see His life as belonging to Himself or to be lived for Himself; He was a steward of that which belonged to God the Father. He taught this life of dependence on God and warned people about the deceitfulness of putting our trust in possessions. Jesus' life was a model of trusting stewardship and surrender. Because

He fully trusted the Father, He was free to surrender all to Him. He gave of Himself. Likewise, the Christlike person surrenders his body, heart, mind, time, money, and energy for God's purposes. To be Christlike is to live this kind of trusting surrender out in a life of stewardship.

If we want to be like Christ, we need to know Jesus better. As we explore these six core characteristics in the chapters that follow, we will see each of these characteristics lived out in Scripture in the life of Jesus. With these in mind, as we practice Spiritual Breathing and cooperate with the Holy Spirit's work in our life, He is working to form and develop these core characteristics in us: this is His work of spiritual formation. Cooperation with the Spirit's work in our life is much easier if we know what He's doing and what He's trying to develop.

Of course, there are more characteristics of Christlikeness than these six, but these are the *core* characteristics. All of the other characteristics we see in the life of Christ and seek to develop in ours come out of these six core characteristics. Let's take, for example, humility, a favorite classical characteristic of Christlikeness. Humility does not come by concentrating on humility but by living out the six core characteristics. If you pursue the core characteristics of Christlikeness, especially the first, third, and fifth (living connected to God, loving others, and serving them), humility comes as a byproduct. Humility happens when we take seriously what it means to love God and love people, not by navel gazing and trying to be humble. Or take patience, a virtue that can only be developed as we love people and serve them.

Exploring each of these core characteristics in Jesus' life will be the subject of the rest of the book. We will examine how they played out in Jesus' life, how the Spirit was at work in Jesus' life, and how He is at work in our life to reproduce these same characteristics in us. We will learn how to more fully cooperate with the Spirit by developing skills and attitudes with the Spirit's help.

We can become more like Christ.

God designed us to be like Christ.

The world needs for us to be like Christ.

The Holy Spirit is working to make us like Christ.

We just need to learn to breathe.

CHAPTER FIVE

Spiritual Breathing

Core Christlike Characteristic: Jesus lived in vital connection with God

The Core Christlike Characteristics start with this first and most important one. All of the other Christlike characteristics come from this foundational source: *Jesus lived in vital connection with God.* This connected, life-giving relationship with God leaps off every page in the Gospels; you can't miss it. The question for you and me is "*how?* How did Jesus live in and maintain this vital connection with God?

Throughout this book I've repeated the phrase *the only way to live is to breathe.* Breathing is the central action of life, even though it is usually ignored. You might say breathing connects us to life. A visit to a hospital or hospice where people are on ventilators, or as it is aptly called, artificial life support, makes this immediately clear.

I've suggested that Jesus practiced a way of living called Spiritual Breathing that was the secret to His remarkable life. Spiritual Breathing is *how* Jesus lived in vital connection with God. In doing so, Jesus modeled a way of living that reflected God's design and dream when He created humanity. When we look at the life of Jesus, we see how God intended our life to be lived: connected to God in an intimate, abundant way.

While He was here on earth Jesus said, "I came to give life, and life more abundantly." God wants us to live this abundant, Christlike life, and many of us have heard the call and want to be like Christ. But there's only one way this will happen: *the only way to live (the Christian life) is to breathe (the Holy Spirit).* We have said that the Holy Spirit is Spiritual Oxygen; only the Holy Spirit can produce the life of Christ in us. In fact, any other way of living is artificial life support which usually keeps us existing but doesn't give us quality of life, abundant life.

The secret to living the Christlike life is learning how to breathe in the Holy Spirit so He transforms our lives. We saw earlier how in the original languages (Hebrew, Aramaic, and Greek) the Bible uses the same word for "Spirit" and for "breath." These words are virtually synonyms. God has built into our world a fascinating parallel between the physical and the spiritual. Just as our physical bodies are kept alive by the physical action of breathing, so our spiritual life is made alive and kept alive by Spiritual Breathing: inhaling the Spirit of God into our lives. As a matter of fact, this beautiful, primordial rhythm of breathing is reflected in much of God's creation.

The Real Circle of Life

Just a few moments of attentiveness to your own breathing reveals the rhythmic, cyclical nature to this action. Take ten seconds right now and notice your breathing. There's a circular pattern to it: you breathe in, you breathe out. You inhale, you exhale. Feel the rhythm? Without the New Age overtones, we understand that the action of breathing is a circle of life. The rhythm of breathing keeps us alive. When breathing stops, life stops.

But it's not just our bodies that reflect this cycle. God has formatted this cyclical, circular rhythm throughout our universe. Have you ever thought about how many things in creation are cyclical and/or circular? Our earth is circular in shape and spins on an invisible axis in a circular motion. We circle around the sun, which creates cycles on earth. We have (at least in Cleveland, Ohio) the cycle of four seasons, year after year after year. Each twenty-four-hour period is a cycle of day and night.

God has also built this cyclical motion into healthy relating and communication. Understanding this communication cycle will help us see what happens in Spiritual Breathing.

Most people have taken communication classes in high school or college or maybe even at their church. No doubt you've seen some version of this communication cycle.

Communication is about speaking and listening in reciprocal, cyclical fashion. If the cycle gets interrupted at any point, communication ceases. The best communication is where the cycle flows freely without break. When we communicate well, we feel connected because communication creates connection.

God wants to live in connection with us, so He creates us to relate and communicate with Him, to connect. God is the great communicator and so He initiates communication with us. God always speaks first. He spoke first in the Garden of Eden; He speaks first in every relationship. No one ever initiates with God. We only seek Him because He has first sought us and extended His grace to us. We are always responders.

Living in Rhythm with God

Throughout history, as people ignored God He has continued to speak. His passion to connect with us led to Him speaking the "Word of God" which was written down and is known today as the Bible. The Bible is God speaking to us, communicating with us, and revealing His heart. In the pages of the Bible, God is seeking connection with us and inviting response. In order to keep the communication cycle going, we must respond. Our response is prayer and worship. We will talk more about the response of worship later. In this chapter we will focus on entering into the rhythm of Spiritual Breathing by examining more closely the communication rhythm God has created: listening to and receiving the Spirit and responding in prayer. This receive-respond cycle corresponds to the inhale-exhale cycle of physical breathing. As we inhale, we receive the Spirit; as we exhale, we respond in prayer.

Spiritual Breathing is listening to, receiving, and absorbing the presence of the Spirit, and responding in prayer. Listening to the Spirit requires first and foremost that we know the primary language in which the Holy Spirit speaks: the Word of God. As we know the Word of God better, we learn how to breathe in the words of life the Spirit is breathing out. We hear His Word then we respond. We inhale His Word then we exhale our prayer response.

This communication circle of Spiritual Breathing is where the Holy Spirit does His work. He not only speaks into us, primarily through the Word, but He is also the one who forms in us our prayer response back to God.

The Holy Spirit is the great facilitator of our relationship to God. This is what Jesus meant in John 16:13-14. Please read these words carefully. It is vital that we understand this primary role of the Holy Spirit.

> But when he, the Spirit of truth, comes, he will guide you into all truth. He will not speak on his own; he will speak only what he hears, and he will tell you what is yet to come. He will bring glory to me by taking from what is mine and making it known to you.

The Holy Spirit doesn't communicate *His* messages, but the Father's and Jesus'. He facilitates communication between God and us, interpreting for us what God is saying. Paul points out the other side of this Spirit-guided communication in Romans 8:26-27:

We do not know what we ought to pray for, but the Spirit himself intercedes for us with groans that words cannot express. And he who searches our hearts knows the mind of the Spirit, because the Spirit intercedes for the saints in accordance with God's will.

In the John 16 passage we see the Holy Spirit facilitating communication between God and us, and in the Romans 8 passage we see the Holy Spirit facilitating communication between us and God. We call this Spiritual Breathing because of the rhythmic nature of the Spirit's work; it is all guided by, facilitated by, filled by the Holy Spirit. The communication cycle of the Word and prayer is where the Spirit breathes and works in our lives. He breathes into us God's truth and He prompts our response back.

Responding to God

How we respond is determined by what He says. If He points out sin in our life, as we breathe in that word of conviction, our proper response is to breathe out repentance. Then God is faithful to forgive (He can be counted on to communicate back to us forgiveness, thus keeping the communication cycle of Spiritual Breathing going), at which point we respond with receiving His grace, breathing in His forgiveness and allowing it to cleanse and purify us. We respond with gratitude, breathing out prayers of thanksgiving, and the Spiritual Breathing as communication with God continues to cycle.

When there is fear in our life, we breathe in His Word not to fear but to trust, so we inhale His truth to us. Our response back is to express trust in Him. We exhale fear and breathe in trust. As we open ourselves to His Spirit and breathe in His Spiritual Oxygen, our fear is replaced by confidence and our anxiety is cleansed like oxygen-rich blood cleanses our body.

Sin, fear and negative attitudes can take a thousand different forms. When the Holy Spirit points out any of these things in our lives, we need to turn to God and take a deep breath and say to Him: "I need to breathe. I need You. Fill me with Your presence and power. Holy Spirit, fill me with life, breathe into me Your life-giving presence." Then just wait. Pay attention. Expect God to come and bring His peace. God is here. Now. Breathe deeply of His presence. Linger as long as you need to; sit quietly and listen for what He may say next. He may lead you to read a Psalm or a passage from the New Testament. He may point out deeper sin or attitudes that are toxic in your life. Agree with Him. Exhale, confess any sin. Then breathe again deeply of His forgiveness and grace. All you need is God. Breathe in His presence.

As we saw earlier, if we want to listen and understand what the Spirit is saying, we must learn the primary language in which He speaks: the Word of God. When we learned in chapter three that the Holy Spirit is the Breath of God, we also saw that God has spoken through His Word; this is His communication to us. So the clearest way for us to hear from God, the clearest way for us to breathe in His spiritual life, is to take in, or breathe in, His Word. God has breathed out His Word, we must breathe it in. Remember 2 Timothy 3:16: "All Scripture is *God-breathed* and is useful for teaching, rebuking, correcting and training in righteousness" (italics added).

As we know the Word of God better, we learn how to breathe in the words of life the Spirit is breathing out. This is how Jesus lived in vital connection with God. He was a man of the Scriptures and a man of prayer. This explains why Jesus was always quoting Scripture. He understood that the primary languages of the Spirit are prayer and the Word of God, so He learned and spoke those languages fluently and never departed from them.

Today, there is a surprising lack of familiarity with the Word of God. This is true in a general way in terms of being familiar with the themes and overall message of the Bible and it is also true in terms of knowing how to properly interpret the Bible. If we want to learn the language of the Holy Spirit in the Word of God, we have to learn how to study and interpret the Word of God. Once we do, it will be much easier to hear and understand what the Spirit is saying.

Let's look more closely at how Jesus lived in this communication circle of Spiritual Breathing, then how we might practice this in our lives. To do that we will look at how Jesus stayed connected to God through the Word first, and then in chapter seven, we'll look at the other cycle of Spiritual Breathing: Jesus' life of prayer.

SECTION TWO

· ·

Loving God

CHAPTER SIX

Living Connected through the Word

Core Christlike Characteristic: Jesus lived connected to God through the Word

Jesus lived in connection with God through the Word in a way that was so vital it literally nourished Him. He said the Word of God was like food for Him (Matthew 4:4). Jesus quoted Scripture with the ease of someone intimately familiar with it. In Matthew's Gospel, three out of the first four times Jesus spoke, He quoted Scripture! In Luke's Gospel, the first three times Jesus spoke, He quoted Scripture, and the fourth time He spoke, He was reading Scripture. Then He sat down and immediately quoted another Scripture, and proceeded to teach and refer to several others. He quoted famous passages. He quoted obscure passages.

When Jesus dialogued with people, He did it around Scripture. When He taught, He taught from the Scriptures. He understood that the Word of God was the language of the Holy Spirit, and when He quoted the Scriptures, He attributed those words to the Words of the Spirit (Mark 12:36). He lived and breathed the Scriptures.

When it came time for Him to die on the cross, what did He do? He quoted Scripture (Psalms 22 and 31)! Luke tells us that His last breath was breathing out Scripture, quoting from Psalm 31:5: "'Father, into your hands I commit my spirit.' When he had said this, he breathed his last" (Luke 23:46). Jesus was a Scripture-saturated man! You cannot overestimate the significance of the Word of God in the life of Jesus.

If we want to become more like Christ, it is vital that we understand more about this connection Jesus had with God through the Spirit and the Word and how to live in that connection ourselves. Connection is about relationship, and Jesus lived in a 24/7 connected relationship with God through the Holy Spirit that was vibrant and dynamic.

Several years ago I was in an intense meeting that required no interruption. As we were getting started the leader asked us all to turn off our mobile phones. We all complied except for one, a sharp business executive in her forties. She began to gently protest that she needed the phone on but would keep it on vibrate.

An interesting power struggle ensued. As we all watched with growing interest, the leader insisted that she turn it off. "You've got to be kidding me!" she pleaded, her eyes nervous and searching. "I always have it on; please, just let me put it on vibrate." The passion and panic in her voice was startling. You would have thought he had asked her to disown her firstborn. Mind you, this wasn't a teenage drama queen; she was an accomplished, seasoned professional. But everybody has their weak spot. For me it's ice cream, for her it was her mobile phone. She was completely flustered at the thought of being "unconnected."

She's not alone. Smart phones have become the umbilical cord connecting us to society. Most people can't imagine life without a mobile phone. You may not be obsessive about having it on all the time, but you want it nearby, available. The reason why is because that's your connection with your family or your job—with your world. Because of our mobile phones, we can stay connected 24/7.

Staying Connected

Staying connected 24/7 is a great idea; in fact it's God's idea. God's design for us is that we never turn off our "mobile phone" with Him, that we never move into a setting where we click the "off" button and say, "Now I'm doing something secular or non-spiritual and so I don't really need connection right now." No, His design and His desire is that we're always living in this 24/7 connection with Him. And once we understand why, we'll never want to be unconnected again.

Jesus lived in a 24/7 connected relationship with God through the Holy Spirit, and He was careful to teach this connection to His disciples. In the first century, the best metaphor for what it meant to be connected was something that was a very frequent sight throughout Israel: vineyards full of grapevine branches. So when Jesus wanted to teach about how He lived in vital connection with God through the Spirit, and how His disciples might do the same, He turned to this metaphor everyone around Him instantly understood. His words are found in John 15.

I am the true vine, and my Father is the gardener.
He cuts off every branch in me that bears no fruit,
while every branch that does bear fruit he prunes
so that it will be even more fruitful. You are already
clean because of the word I have spoken to you.
Remain in me, and I will remain in you. No branch
can bear fruit by itself; it must remain in the vine.
Neither can you bear fruit unless you remain in
me. I am the vine; you are the branches. If a man
remains in me and I in him, he will bear much fruit;
apart from me you can do nothing. If anyone does
not remain in me, he is like a branch that is thrown
away and withers; such branches are picked up,
thrown into the fire and burned. If you remain in
me and my words remain in you, ask whatever
you wish, and it will be given you. This is to my
Father's glory, that you bear much fruit, showing
yourselves to be my disciples.

As Jesus described what it meant to live in vital union with God, He set up the metaphor by identifying roles immediately. He is the vine and we who are His disciples are the branches on the vine. God the Father is the gardener, meaning He oversees the process of nurturing the plants and producing an abundant harvest. As the gardener, He obviously means business. The next verses help us see that this is more than just a nice little story. If we don't remain in the vine, things don't go well for us. "Cut off" and "burned in the fire" (v. 6) are clearly things we want to avoid.

God intends for disciples to be fruitful. It is abundantly clear what we have to do in order to bear fruit. His next words are simple and plain: "remain in the vine." Eight times in this short passage of Scripture, Jesus uses this word "remain," indicating its importance.

So what does it mean to "remain in the vine"? It means to *stay connected, keep the connection happening.* When we follow the simple command of "remaining," Jesus says "we will bear much fruit." This fruit is typically seen as the fruit of the Holy Spirit that Paul talks about in Galatians 5:22-23: "love, joy, peace, patience, kindness, goodness, faithfulness, gentleness and self-control." The fruit could also be reproducing other Christlike disciples. Either way, at the very least, the fruit of the Christ vine is the Christ life flowing through those who are connected. This is a picture of becoming more like Christ.

So how do we stay connected? Jesus begins to answer that question the last time He uses the word "remain" in verse 7: "If my words remain in you." This verse is very similar to what Jesus said in John 8:31 (NASB): "If you continue in My word, then you are truly disciples of Mine." While one can see the similarity in English, it is even more striking in Greek. The word "continue" in John 8:31 and the word "remain" in John 15 are both the same Greek word: *meno.* It means "to continue to stay in, to abide, to dwell deeply." When you connect it to the vine imagery, it means "to continue to stay connected in a life-giving way."

So in John 15:7 we have "if my words continue to stay in you in a life-giving way like a branch is connected into the vine, then you will bear much fruit"; and in John 8:31 we have "if you continue to stay connected in a life-giving way to my Word, then you are my disciples." Both verses emphasize the concept of "staying connected" and both verses call us to "stay connected" to the same thing: the Word of Jesus.

Staying connected to the vine, Jesus, happens as we stay connected to His Word. But it's not just staying connected any old way. We are to "continue to stay connected in a life-giving way" to the Word of God. There's a way of reading the Bible and even memorizing it that is rote and of no value. There's also a way of reading the Bible that is "staying connected in a life-giving way"; it's a part of the Spiritual Breathing process. Before we explain how to do that, let's finish the verse in John 8:31. Jesus said if we continue in the Word of God, "then you are My disciples."

Re-discovering the Definition of a Disciple

What is a disciple?

In the first century, "disciple" had a very well-known meaning. Throughout Israel, a respected spiritual teacher was called a rabbi, and every rabbi had a group of disciples. The rabbis were well-known and it was an honor to be admitted into discipleship by the most popular rabbis. In fact, the most popular ones had waiting lists. Rabbis didn't go looking for disciples; it was the other way around. It was common to see little circles of disciples gathered around their rabbi as he walked and taught or sat on a large stone with his disciples at his feet. The New Testament records that John the Baptist had disciples and the Pharisees had disciples. All disciples did three major things; each of these three related to each other, and these activities form the core of the meaning of the word.

The first and most basic thing a disciple did was to *follow*. A disciple was a follower of a rabbi. They literally followed the rabbi around the countryside, through the villages and cities, ate with the rabbi, and sometimes slept in the same quarters or nearby the rabbi. A disciple was a follower. You see this very clearly in the Gospels. Everywhere Jesus went, the disciples followed; that's what disciples do. You rarely see Jesus mentioned in the Gospels without the disciples nearby. They were always around.

The disciple would follow the rabbi around for a very particular reason, and that reason was to *learn* from the rabbi. A disciple is "a learner, a student, a pupil." They followed the rabbi to learn his teachings, to learn his philosophy, to learn his way of life. This was a very effective way to teach as the old adage "some things are better caught than taught" was demonstrated daily in the pedagogy of the rabbis.

But the following that led to the learning didn't end there. The goal of every disciple was to *become* more like the rabbi. A disciple is a "becomer." Luke 6:40 says, "A disciple is not above his teacher, but everyone when he is fully trained will be like his teacher."

So a disciple is a follower, a learner, and a becomer. If you put these all together, you get a full definition: "a disciple is a *follower* on a *learning* journey of *becoming* like his master." We are disciples of Jesus, following Him in order to learn from Him so that we might become more like Him.

Now let's go back to John 8:31 and plug in our definition of disciple to complete the very important truth Jesus was communicating:

If you continue in My word, then you are truly disciples of Mine.

means,

If you stay connected in a life-giving way to the Word, then you will be followers on a learning journey of becoming like Jesus.

Something vital and life-giving happens in the process of staying in the Word that directly affects our ability as disciples to become like Jesus. You don't work your way into Christlikeness; you remain in the vine and the Spirit of God—the Christ life—flows into you, and as you follow and learn you become more like Christ. We are going to become more like Christ because the life of Christ is flowing in us, not because we're sweating and working hard and gritting our teeth while repeating "I want to be more like Jesus." We're followers who are on this learning journey of becoming like Him as His life flows into us.

How does this happen? How does being in the Word lead to following, learning, and becoming like Jesus? This is the beauty of the vine and branches metaphor Jesus chose to use in John 15. Staying connected in a life-giving way *transfers the life of the vine* into the life of the branch, just as breathing transfers the life-giving oxygen into our bodies. Remember Jesus is divine, we are da'branch. The "life" in the "Christ vine" that flows into the branches is the Holy Spirit. Though Jesus doesn't spell it out here, He makes it crystal clear in John 6:63 that "The Spirit gives life . . . the *words* I have spoken to you are *spirit* and they are *life*" (italics added).

Holy Spirit Induced Christlikeness

Throughout the Bible, the Spirit is pictured as bringing the "life" of God to people: the Spirit gives life. As we stay connected to the Word in a life-giving way, the life of the vine, the Spirit and life of Jesus, gets transferred into us, His disciples! The life is drawn out of the vine and transferred into the branch. This process of "drawing out" is called *induction*. To apply this inductive process to us, follow the next sentence very carefully. The *life* of the vine (the Spirit and life of Christ) produces the *fruit* of the vine (Christlikeness) through the *branches* (you and me), followers and learners becoming like Jesus. This process is Holy Spirit-induced Christlikeness, Jesus' goal of discipleship for you and me. Just as Jesus lived in vital connection with God, so He invites us into this same kind of Holy Spirit-induced life.

But this Holy Spirit-induced Christlikeness that Jesus is talking about isn't a random, haphazard process; it comes about in a very specific way. The kind of Christ-life that is pictured here is life drawn from being connected to the Word in a life-giving way. It is absolutely essential that we grasp what Jesus is saying here. There is a way of connecting to the Word in a life-giving way that brings Christ's life into our life. The same inductive process described in the vine-branch transfer can be applied directly to our study of the Word of God; it's literally called the inductive Bible study method. It has been taught in different ways by different names throughout the years (Precept studies may be the most popular version of it today), but the core of the method is this idea of "drawing out" the life-giving truths of the Word of God.

This is why inductive Bible study is so powerful, because we're drawing out the life of the Word of God through a specific process of studying Scripture. If you've never been introduced to this life-giving way of studying the Bible, I've excerpted it out of this chapter into Appendix A. Turn there and I will teach it to you now. It's one of the most important skills you will ever learn.

Breathing Example

One of the ways I use this pattern of breathing God's Word into my life is through the process of how I write sermons as a pastor. I typically work through a book of the Bible one passage at a time, and each week as I come to the next section of Scripture, I habitually practice Spiritual Breathing. I ask God to breathe into me understanding of His Word. I pray prayers like: "Holy Spirit, what does this verse mean? Breathe into me understanding. Breathe into me the life of Your Word. Open the eyes of my heart to the wonderful truths in Your Word." As I am studying, I am practicing Spiritual Breathing, what I call prayerful exegesis, dialoguing with God throughout the process. (For you pastors, scholars and students, I wrote my doctoral thesis on this process of prayerful exegesis. The thesis is entitled "Proclaiming What We've Seen and Heard: The Role of Prayer in Hermeneutics for Homiletics.") The most exciting hours of my week are usually these moments of sensing God breathing into me insight and understanding. I feel His presence, receive His life and am filled with His power. By the time the weekend rolls around I am bursting at the seams, full of God's truth, power and presence and I can't wait to share with my people what God has breathed into me that week!

Sometimes the process of hearing God speak through His Word is long and hard. Working through centuries of cultural and semantic barriers is one challenge and recognizing my interpretive biases is yet another. Other times, God just speaks so clearly and simply it's impossible to miss. I was reading Luke 14 the other day and came across verses 12-14 where Jesus says, "When you give a luncheon or dinner, do not invite your friends, your brothers or relatives, or your rich neighbors; if you do, they may invite you back and so you will be repaid. [13] But when you give a banquet, invite the poor, the crippled, the lame, the blind, [14] and you will be blessed."

As I was reading I sensed the Holy Spirit simply say, "do this." It was just two simple words that He breathed into my spirit, but I began to get excited. I thought, "yes, of course! That would be awesome. Let's just do exactly what Jesus said: give a banquet for the poor, crippled, lame and blind! Why didn't I think of this before?" So I shared the idea with some others and they got pumped. Then I shared it with another group and they were all over it. Next thing I know we've got thirty people in a room planning how we can pull this off. This book went to press while we are still in the planning stages of the banquet. I can't wait to see it all come together, but it all started with the Holy Spirit and the Word of God.

Breathing Exercise

God wants to lead us by His Holy Spirit to live connected to Him through the power of His Word. He invites us into knowing Him through reading and meditating on His Word and receiving His life-giving presence and power. As you practice Spiritual Breathing, pay attention to the breathing in and breathing out cycle, using the natural rhythm of your breathing to focus your prayers.

Here is some language to guide our Spiritual Breathing as we live connected to God through His Word:

- As we breathe in, we want to receive the Holy Spirit and say: *"Holy Spirit, breathe in me insight into the Scriptures; open my eyes to see."*
- As we breathe out, we want to remove any sin or toxins and say: *"I confess my lack of living in connection with You."*
- As we breathe in, we want to receive the Holy Spirit and say: *"Holy Spirit, I receive Your life-giving truth into my life."*
- As we breathe out, we want to thank God and say: *"Holy Spirit, thank You for your presence and power."*

Alternate words as we breathe in:

> *"Holy Spirit, breathe in me the Word of God."*
> *"Holy Spirit, breathe in me understanding."*
> *"Holy Spirit, breathe in me love for Your Word."*
> *"Holy Spirit, breathe in me the desire to obey Your Word."*

Alternate words as we breathe out:

> *"I confess my neglect of Your Word."*
> *"I confess my sin of disobedience."*
> *"I confess my sin of being a hearer only and not a doer of Your Word."*
> *"I confess my resistance to Your truth."*

Feel free to add, elaborate, or edit as needed. Remember, the Holy Spirit wants to shape our hearts and minds with His Word as He makes us more like Christ. We just need to learn to *breathe.*

CHAPTER SEVEN

Living Connected through Prayer

Core Christlike Characteristic: Jesus Lived Connected to God through Prayer

We've seen how Jesus stayed in connection with God through the Word. Now let's look more closely at how He lived in connection with God through prayer. Prayer is a conversation with God, a dialogue where God speaks to us and we speak to Him. Healthy communication is a reciprocal exercise that creates a circular motion of give and take, speaking and listening. In chapter six we learned about connecting to God through the Word, and Appendix A models how to study the Word of God prayerfully. We saw that prayerful study of God's Word is the best way of listening to God. We complete this communication circle between God and us as we respond in prayer. I read the Word to hear from God, that's God speaking; and then I complete this cycle as I respond back to Him in prayer. So prayer is a circle, a dance, an ongoing rhythmic conversation with God. We want to learn to weave biblical, Christlike prayer throughout the rhythms and cycles of our day.

In preparation for a sermon I was writing on prayer, I emailed the people in our church a simple question: what are the reasons people don't pray? The response blew me away. The response was easily ten times that of previous similar email requests. I learned and grew from their insights and wept and marveled at their stories.

Far and away the number one reason was that people were "too busy to pray." Life was too crazy, their schedule was too full, their pace too fast, and they just couldn't find time to squeeze it in. Some people went on to add, "But everyone finds time for what is most important, so it's really an excuse, not a reason."

Have you noticed that when we feel the need urgently enough, we suddenly find time to pray? When we desperately need a job, or direction, or there is an urgent health concern, people who were once too busy find the time to pray. Maybe the number one reason why people don't pray is really "we don't feel the need urgently enough."

The second reason was "unanswered prayer." What they meant, of course, was that prayers weren't answered the way they wanted. God always answers prayer; He just doesn't always answer it the way we want. The root cause of this one is a misperception of prayer, which includes a misperception of God.

Misperceptions of Prayer

Some people view prayer like a vending machine. God is the Great Vending Machine in the Sky, and when we put the right amount of money in and choose what we want, we expect our answer to come spiraling out. If it doesn't, we try it again, bang on the machine and, if no one is looking, give it a kick and walk away.

Others view prayer like some Aladdin genie lamp. If we say the right words, meaning if we pray the Scriptures with faith, God will come out and is obligated to give us what we request.

Then there are those who view prayer as a spiritual treadmill. We know prayer is good for us, and so we dutifully get on the treadmill and do our time, slogging away the minutes, dreading every moment of it, but reminding ourselves that this is what you have to do if you want to be a good Christian.

I am always deeply saddened by those in the fourth category: those who view prayer as coming before an angry judge. We slink up to the towering bench and peer up at a scowling, angry face, gavel poised in irritated anticipation. The loud voice behind the bench booms "What do you want now? Can't you see I'm busy?" The mere thought of approaching the judge brings out the cowering scarecrow in us all.

Your perception of God is the single most determining factor in your relationship with Him. The first words of A.W. Tozer's book *Knowledge of the Holy* are revealing: "What comes into our minds when we think about God is the most important thing about us." Who you perceive God to be determines how you relate to Him. If you view God as distant and uninterested or angry, that will dramatically affect how (or if) you pray. If you view prayer as a vending machine or genie lamp, then when you don't get what you want, you conclude that prayer doesn't work and you give up.

What we need is a new picture of prayer, a new image that is more representative of how Jesus viewed prayer. For

Jesus, prayer was simply a conversation with His Father. Instead of the vending machine, genie lamp, treadmill, or angry judge, I invite you to picture prayer as sitting down at a coffee shop with a very good friend or family member and talking about what is on your heart. Granted, He's a Very Big Friend and a Holy, Perfect Friend; it's not like we are equals, but we are friends. We are family. Prayer is this very natural, relational conversation with God.

Learning to Pray Like Jesus

When you study prayer in the life of Jesus, one of the first things that stands out is the variety and richness of His prayer life. Jesus is pictured as getting up early and praying first thing in the morning, but it doesn't stop there. He prays spontaneously right in the middle of a teaching time with His disciples. Prompted by the Holy Spirit, Jesus would stop in the middle of what He was doing and pray. Luke 10 shows us one of these times. Notice the spontaneous and Spirit-led nature of this moment: "At that time Jesus, full of joy through the Holy Spirit, said, 'I praise you, Father, Lord of heaven and earth, because you have hidden these things from the wise and learned, and revealed them to little children. Yes, Father, for this was your good pleasure'" (Luke 10:21).

New Testament scholar Joachim Jeremias did a study on Jesus as a first-century Jew, comparing the Gospels and Judaism, and concluded that Jesus almost assuredly practiced the regular morning, noon, and evening prayer times of the faithful Jew. In addition to early morning, spontaneous, and regular prayer times, Jesus is pictured several times as praying all night.

Jesus prayed in solitude, He prayed in public, and He prayed in a small group. As Jesus lived in intimate connection with the Father through the Holy Spirit, He breathed out prayers of all kinds at all times. Jesus' disciples noticed this life of connection and prayer and asked Him to teach them how to pray (Luke 11:1). His response has become known as the Lord's Prayer but is probably better titled the Disciples' Prayer since this was the prayer He taught His disciples. I have prayed this prayer He taught His disciples for many years. I've read books and articles on it. I've studied it and preached sermons on it. But I had never seen what He was about to show me.

During a time in my prayer life that was dry and routine, I cried out to the Lord to revitalize my prayer life. This by the way is the best way to deal with those dry prayer times: ask God for renewal and renovation. Most people who struggle with prayer fit into one of these categories:

- Those who don't know how to pray need instruction
- Those who wander and daydream need organization
- Those whose prayer life is dry need renovation

I don't know where you are today, but when Jesus taught His disciples this prayer, He covered all the bases. If you belong to the first group, either because you're a new Christian or because no one has ever taught you how to pray, Jesus provides some great instruction in this lesson on prayer.

If you know how to pray but find yourself wandering and daydreaming during your prayer time, it might be because you don't have a clear structure in which to pray. Scholars argue over whether Jesus intended this prayer to be repeated word for word or whether it was more of a pattern, a structure with which to organize prayer concerns, kind of like a prayer outline. I say there's nothing to argue about: it's both. (It's amazing how often that's the right answer!) Though I lean more towards thinking Jesus was giving His disciples a prayer pattern or outline of sorts, I believe this is a prayer that can be prayed just as it is without elaboration with great profit.

If you find yourself, as I did, where your prayer life is dry, this new way of praying can bring renovation and renewal to your prayer life. Wherever you are in your prayer journey as you read this page, I am stopping right now to pray for you (in anticipation that someone will read this) that God will meet you and take your prayer life to the next level. I pray that because of a more intimate and abundant life of prayer, you will become more like Christ.

This was by no means the only season in my life where my prayer life has gotten really dry, but it was the most memorable—primarily because of how it ended! The models I was using or the way I was praying became so routine and dry that I didn't want to pray. The structure of my prayer time (and probably the condition of my heart) was hindering me from going deeper in my relationship with God. So I just cried out to God for revival. I stopped, took a deep breath and said "Holy Spirit, breathe into me

Your presence. Fill me with Your life. I receive Your presence into my life again. Revive me, Lord."

I also needed to prepare a teaching on prayer, and I knew I couldn't teach out of a dry heart. I needed God to breathe into me new life. I needed God to breathe into me direction. I needed God to breathe into me His words.

Again, I practiced Spiritual Breathing and prayed these simple words: "fill me with Your presence. I receive You now." Soon, I sensed God directing me to this famous prayer that Jesus taught His disciples, and my first reaction was "been there, done that." Fortunately I obeyed, and what God began to show me in the next moments revolutionized my prayer life.

As I studied the prayer in Matthew's version (6:9-13) I began to see a pattern I had never noticed before, but as it became clearer I got more and more excited about it. Jesus was teaching a prayer pattern that lined up perfectly with how He lived His life! I shouldn't have been surprised but I was. I had never noticed this before. As we will see later on, Jesus could be summarized as one who practiced *loving God*, *loving people*, and *living surrendered*. So it only makes sense that we should see these same themes in the prayer He taught His disciples to pray.

Loving God

Jesus begins the prayer in a way that would have shocked any good Jew living in the first century. When He addressed God as "Father," it broke all conventional patterns of prayer. Jesus didn't just respect God; He loved Him intimately, and it showed in the way He addressed God in His prayer.

Jews were a praying people, and they had prayers for just about every occasion. About 95 percent of the prayers started the same way: "Blessed are You Lord our God, King of the Universe." When you prayed, you addressed God with titles and reverent language that was representative of His lofty position. That kind of praying was good, it was proper, it was respectful. But it also tended to be religious. Here comes Jesus, and instead of practicing religion He's cultivating relationship. This comes out in the way He addresses God as "Father."

Jesus' language introduced a level of intimacy and immediacy that moved prayer into much more of a relational role than a religious role. This would have offended many of the religious rulers of Jesus' day. Even more scandalous is the actual word Jesus would have used. Since He was probably praying in Aramaic, He would have used the word "Abba" as He did in other places where the Aramaic was not translated into Greek. Abba meant "Daddy" or "loving Father" and was a term of love and intimacy and family. By using this word, Abba, it was as if Jesus was saying "I love You, Daddy." Now that kind of language is embarrassing to proper religious people. It feels irreverent, inappropriate, even sacrilegious. Nobody addressed God as Daddy—it was unheard of!

Much has been written on Jesus' use of the word Abba in addressing God. It speaks volumes about how Jesus perceived God and—since He is teaching His disciples here—how He invites us to see God. Your view of God, your perception of God, is the single most determining factor in your prayer life. For some of you, you will never learn "a new way to pray" until you unlearn your conception of God and discover what He is really like. Your new way to pray starts with a new way of viewing God.

What is the first thing Jesus communicates with the first words of His prayer? Prayer is a time to love God, a time to cultivate our relationship with Him. Come to Him as a child comes to his loving father, eager, trusting, expressive, and confident in his love. I hope prayer is a time for you to love on God, to tell Him how much you love Him, to express your adoration for who He is. While He is holy, transcendent, sovereign, and all-powerful, for Jesus He was first of all Daddy! As Jesus expresses His love for God in prayer, it reveals four things about how Jesus saw prayer. These four ways of loving God in prayer can renew your prayer life and make it more like Christ's:

1. **Prayer is a time to cultivate our relationship with God.**

   For Jesus, prayer wasn't about being religious, it was about relationship. He doesn't "say His prayers," He talks to God. Prayer is a part of Spiritual Breathing and it revitalizes and renews our relationship with God. Prayer is communion, a time to express love, to cultivate intimacy, to strengthen our relationship with God.

2. **Prayer is a time to communicate with God.**

   The most important thing every relationship needs is communication. This is true for our earthly relationships and our relationship with God. Connection and intimacy come through communication. When we communicate, we feel connected. Jesus didn't take for granted the intimate union He had with God; He nurtured it by communication.

3. **Prayer is a time to calibrate our life to God.**

In Mark 4:19 Jesus said that "the worries of this life, the deceitfulness of wealth and the desires for other things come in and choke the word of God" in our life and we lose our way and get off track. Prayer is a time to align and realign our heart and priorities with God's.

4. **Prayer is a time to celebrate the character of God.**

This is seen in the very next words Jesus teaches His disciples to pray: "hallowed be your name." To hallow is to sanctify, to honor God with recognition of His holiness; this is celebrating God's character. God is holy. His name reveals His character. This is true for all the names of God. The biblical names for God describe His nature and His character. Jesus is pointing to celebrating God by meditating on His character revealed in His name. I have listed below some of the more popular Old Testament names for God. Use this partial list in your time of prayer to remind you of the reasons God is worthy of our love. Meditate on the meaning of each name, celebrating who He is, what He has done, and what He will yet do on your behalf.

Jehovah (Hebrew-YHWH): The Self-Existent One

"God said to Moses 'I Am Who I Am.'"—Exodus 3:14;
"O LORD, our LORD, how Majestic is Your name!"—Psalm 8:1

Jehovah-Rohi: The Lord Is My Shepherd

"The LORD is my shepherd I shall not want."—Psalm 23:1

Jehovah-Jireh: My Provider

"So Abraham called that place [Jehovah Jireh] The LORD Will Provide. And to this day it is said, 'On the mountain of the LORD it will be provided.'"—Genesis 22:14

Jehovah-Mekoddishkem: The Lord Who Sanctifies You

"Consecrate yourselves and be holy because I am the LORD your God. Keep my decrees and follow them. I am the Lord your God who sanctifies you [makes you holy]."—Leviticus 20:7-8

Jehovah-Rapha: The Lord Who Heals

"I am the LORD, who heals you."—Exodus 15:26
"He heals the brokenhearted and binds up their wounds."
—Psalm 147:3

Jehovah-Shalom: The Lord Is Your Peace

"So Gideon built an altar to the LORD there and called it The LORD is Peace."—Judges 6:24

Jehovah-Tsidkenu: The Lord Our Righteousness

"This is the name by which He will be called Jehovah Tsidkenu-The LORD our Righteousness."—Jeremiah 23:6

Elohim: God the Creator

"Do you not know? Have you not heard? The LORD is the everlasting God, the Creator of the ends of the earth. He will not grow tired or weary, and his understanding no one can fathom."—Isaiah 40:28

El Elyon: The Sovereign Ruler of All the Universe

"I will be glad and rejoice in you; I will sing praise to your name, O Most High."—Psalm 9:2

El Shaddai: Almighty, All Powerful, and All Sufficient

"I Am God Almighty; walk before me and be blameless. I will confirm my covenant between me and you and will greatly increase your numbers."—Genesis 17:1-2

Meditating on the names of God is a powerful exercise. As we pray the names of God, God reveals more of His character and power in our lives.

I have a friend who was praying some of these names when he was going through a difficult time recently. Feeling burdened and stressed, he just began to pray through the names of God: "Lord, You're my healer." "Lord, You're here, present with me now." "Lord, You are my provider." As he prayed, he said he could feel the power and presence of God rise in him, strengthening him, empowering him to face extremely challenging circumstances. He grew like crazy during that time and still looks back on the morning of just praying the names of God with awe and gratitude.

Living Surrendered

The next phrase Jesus teaches is a prayer of surrender. The first word in the phrase may be the most important: "your." Notice what Jesus prays: "<u>your</u> kingdom come, <u>your</u> will be done." There's nothing in His prayer about "what I want, what I need, what I want God to do for me." It's not "<u>my</u> kingdom come, <u>my</u> will be done." Right out of the gate Jesus is teaching us to surrender what we want and to surrender to what God wants. It's a paradigm shift of huge proportions compared to the way most people pray. Jesus is teaching a prayer of living surrendered. Most people don't get very far into their prayers before they are telling God what they want, what they need. It's all about me, my, mine, I. Jesus is teaching us to start with surrender: surrender the "me and mine" to "you and yours." If we dig a little deeper, we'll find there are three acts of surrender in this prayer.

The first act of surrender is indicated by the very next word in Jesus' prayer: "kingdom." Kingdom is a leadership word. "Your kingdom come" has to do with leadership. Kingdom matters are leadership matters. So Jesus is teaching His disciples, "when you pray to God, surrender to His leadership." Those very words are a stumbling block for some of us. We are wired to say "my kingdom come, my will be done." To surrender, to say "your kingdom come, your will be done," is giving up control. We are afraid to surrender the leadership of our lives to anyone else; it feels like defeat, like we are losing. And in a sense we are. We are losing control, surrendering control, to another. But God's leadership is not a leadership that takes advantage of us.

One of the greatest leaders in Israel's history was Moses. And like all leaders that God uses in a great way, they must learn surrender. Moses learned some hard lessons, but one he never forgot was to what kind of leader he was surrendering. In Exodus 15:13 he says of God: "In your *unfailing love you will lead* the people you have redeemed" (italics added). God's leadership is unique in that the driving characteristic of His leadership is love. When Jesus teaches the disciples to surrender the leadership of their lives to God, He is teaching them to surrender to the *loving* leadership of God: the God we address as "loving Father."

We noted that "kingdom" is a leadership word, but what exactly are we surrendering? We are surrendering our kingdom to His kingdom. What does that mean? Where is our kingdom? In Luke 17:21 Jesus says, ". . . the kingdom of God is within you" meaning in your heart. Our heart is the place of leadership of our life. Our "kingdom" is in our heart. Remember the prayer of surrender Paul referred to in Romans 10:10? He said to "confess with your mouth" and "believe in your heart." That's a prayer of surrendering the leadership of your heart to God. When Jesus teaches His disciples to pray "your kingdom come" He is teaching us to surrender our heart to God's loving leadership.

1. Surrender Your Heart to His Loving Leadership

When I was a kid, we used to sing a song in church that called us to "surrender all the kingdoms of my heart." That's part of the idea of the words "your kingdom come." The natural inclination of my heart is to want my kingdom, my plans, my way to be done, so when I pray the words "your kingdom come," I am surrendering my heart and all the kingdoms in my heart that are rivals to God's kingdom.

Jesus' prayer of surrender has two parts. After we pray "your kingdom come," we pray "your will be done." Here we specifically do what the verse says: we surrender our will. We are presenting our will to God and saying "You lead me. I recognize that I have a will, but I surrender it to Yours. I want Your will to be done in my life."

Remember Jesus' last night on earth before the cross? He was in the Garden of Gethsemane and these were His very words, "not my will but yours be done." One of the things I love about Jesus is that He doesn't teach us to do something He's not doing Himself. This is a prayer He is teaching His disciples as they are training to be like Him. Luke 6:40 says that "when a disciple is fully trained, he will be like his master." This is a disciple-training-to-be-like-Christ prayer. He teaches us to surrender our will to God's leadership because that's what He does.

When Jesus prayed this prayer of surrender in the Garden of Gethsemane, He was able to pray it because He practiced living surrendered. This is one of the places where Jesus uses the name Abba: "Abba, Father, not my will but yours be done." I exhale my desire to go my way and I inhale God's will, God's way. I surrender. This act of surrender is a bold act of trust. I am putting my trust in God; I am placing my confidence in His trustworthiness. I am declaring that His leadership, His direction, is trustworthy. This is the second act of surrender in these verses:

2. Surrender Your Will to His Trustworthy Leadership

To surrender my will to God's is to align me with God's will and God's heart. I begin to have the mind of Christ as I align my will with God's. Surrendering to His loving, trustworthy leadership aligns me with heaven's priorities and heaven's perspective. Jesus prays that God's will be done "on earth as it is in heaven." I surrender my will so that my life reflects heaven's priorities. There's no battle of the wills here. Just as in heaven where God's will is perfectly done, I surrender my will so His will is done here, in my life, the same way. I want my life on earth to be a demonstration of the will of God each day, every day. So it's no surprise then that the very next words, "Give us this day . . . ," have to do with the day-to-day living out of this surrender. We are saying, "Today, I want to live for You. Today I surrender my heart and my will to You." This leads us to our third act of surrender:

3. Surrender Your Day to His Sovereign Leadership

Every day we should pray this prayer of surrender: "Lead me this day, Lord. I surrender this day to You." We surrender to God's loving, trustworthy leadership because He is our sovereign Lord. We acknowledge God's sovereign right to rule our lives as we surrender to His sovereignty. We pray, "You're in charge today. I surrender my heart and my will TODAY, all day, throughout the day."

For years I have practiced a simple way of surrendering to the Lord at the beginning of my day. I roll out of bed and land on my knees and pray: "Lord, today I want to love

You, love people, and live surrendered. Help me to love You with all my heart, soul, mind, and strength; help me to love people the way Jesus did; and help me to live a 'not my will but Yours be done' kind of day. Amen." Starting my day by surrendering it to God and hearing myself say to Him "I want to love You, love people, and live surrendered" helps me get off on the right foot. Perhaps you might try it tomorrow morning. And then the next morning, and the next . . . It could revolutionize your life.

Loving People

I believe it's worth repeating what we noticed above, that when Jesus was teaching His disciples how to pray, He never taught them to pray for themselves; there's not a "me" or "I" in the prayer. Instead He taught them to prayer in the third person plural, using "us" and "we" and "our." Notice how many times these words appear in these short verses:

> Give **us** today **our** daily bread. Forgive **us our** debts, as **we** also have forgiven **our** debtors. And lead **us** not into temptation, but deliver **us** from the evil one.

Jesus is teaching His disciples to pray what I call "Us and We Prayers." The same Jesus who said the two greatest commandments were "love God" and "love people" embedded in the prayer He taught His disciples the same two ideas: treasure the name of God, revel in His character that His names reveal, and then move onto praying for people, the "we's" and "us's."

The first church I pastored was in Pennsylvania near Philadelphia, and many of the people there spoke in plurals. They would say things like: "How are yous doing?" or "Wees going for ice cream after church, yous want to come along?" Besides the fact that the concept of asking me if I want to go get some ice cream was silly (it's like asking someone if you'd like to breathe), the funnier part was the "wees" and "yous." Jesus is teaching us to pray in "wees" and "yous." Pray plural. In other words, pray for others. Why? Because praying for someone is one of the purest ways to love someone. To pray for a person is to practice loving that person.

Jesus taught three "Us and We Prayers" in this passage:

1. **Give Us What We Need.**

   God invites us to bring to Him our needs. Pray for the needs of your family, your church, and your country. James 4:2 says, "You do not have because you do not ask God."

2. **Forgive Us When We Sin.**

   We sin against each other so it's "us" and "we" that need to forgive and be forgiven.

3. **Deliver Us From the Evil One.**

   Again, notice how this is an "us" prayer. This is because Satan attacks the body of Christ, the church. One of the ways he attacks us is by trying to break up the "we-ness" of the church. It's a classic strategy: divide and conquer. This is why Jesus not only teaches His disciples this prayer, but He prays the very same prayer Himself in John 17, the night before He died. In John 17:9 Jesus prays for us, the church: "I pray for them. I am not praying for the world, but for those you have given me, for they are yours." What did He pray for us? "My prayer is not that you take them out of the world but that you protect them from the evil one" (John 17:15).

Notice how similar this prayer is to the one He taught His disciples to pray in Matthew 6. What is the evil one, Satan, trying to do? Verse 23 gives us our answer as Jesus prays for the unity of the church. If more churches prayed for unity, we would be praying like Christ, God would answer our prayer, and the evil one's attacks against the church would be defeated. We are the church, and Jesus teaches us to pray for "us."

These aren't the only prayers Jesus prayed and taught us to pray. In addition to "Us and We Prayers" there are "Other-Centered Prayers."

Other-Centered Prayers

Our ability to pray for others flows from our understanding of God's love for us and knowing that we are deeply loved by Him. Loving God and living in the light of His nature and character makes it possible to love people as God would have us to love them. When we are secure in our love relationship with God, we will love people better.

One of the reasons you may find yourself not praying for people is because you've not really learned yet to receive and to bask in the love of God for you. Since you haven't received grace and love to a great extent, you don't have much grace and love to give. Jesus said "freely you've received, now freely give." When you try to love out of your own strength, it doesn't work; you run out. You get tired of people. You get frustrated with people. You get short with people. You get short with people. You get short with people. You get upset when people repeat themselves. When you bask in the love of God and realize how much He loves you, and your identity in Christ is clear, it births love in you for other people. If you find yourself short on love, spend some time breathing in and receiving God's love, breathing in and receiving God's grace. You will find that breathing in God's love for you will birth love for others in you.

As you pray for others, don't forget to pray for people who persecute you and wrong you. This is one of the areas where we are least Christlike. Jesus said specifically, "Pray for those who persecute you" (Matthew 5:44). Maybe you've never done this before. Try it. God will do something in you as you pray for those who persecute you or hurt you. (See Luke 6:27-28 in the NLT.) The Holy Spirit will give you a love for people that is beyond your own ability, but it will only happen as you pray, obey, and cooperate with Him.

Jesus specifically prayed for pre-Christians, for those who don't believe now but will (John 17:20). As we will see in chapter ten, to be like Christ is to intentionally reach out in love to those who are outside the body of Christ, to pray for them, to show them God's love, and to share the Good News with them. Christlike people regularly pray for specific people to come to faith.

In addition to the other-centered prayers of Jesus, the New Testament records numerous other prayers or people for whom we are called to pray. Paul says in Ephesians 6:18 (CEV), "Never stop praying, especially for others." These "others" include:

- Preachers of the gospel (Ephesians 6:19-20)
- Civil leaders (1 Timothy 2:1-2)
- Family, friends, coworkers (Philemon 1-6)
- Needy and hurting (James 5:14)

Pray for the outcast, for those who are poor. Pray for people who are discouraged. Pray for your family, your neighbors, those you work with, your pastors, your church, your leaders. Pray the Scriptures. This is something I love to do. One of my favorite scriptures to pray is from Ephesians 1:16-19:

> *I have not stopped giving thanks for you, remembering you in my prayers. I keep asking that the God of our Lord Jesus Christ, the glorious Father, may give you the Spirit of wisdom and revelation, so that you may know him better. I pray also that the eyes of your heart may be enlightened in order that you may know the hope to which he has called you, the riches of his glorious inheritance in the saints, and his incomparably great power for us who believe.*

When we are praying for others, we are demonstrating God's character in our lives; we are demonstrating love for others. When we are praying for others, we are responding to the promptings of the Holy Spirit living in us and bringing others and their needs to the feet of our sovereign God.

The three most important prayers you can pray for people are:

1. That they may surrender to Jesus Christ.
   "I pray for those who will believe." John 17:20a
2. That they may know God better.
   "I pray . . . that you may know him better."
   Ephesians 1:17
3. That they may become more like Christ.
   "I pray that out of his glorious riches he may strengthen you with power through his Spirit in your inner being, so that Christ may dwell in your hearts through faith . . . that you may be filled to the measure of all the fullness of God." Ephesians 3:16-19

To review, we can see how these three themes of *loving God, loving people*, and *living surrendered* correspond to the prayer Jesus taught His disciples to pray:

Loving God:	Our Father in heaven, hallowed be your name
Loving People:	Give us today our daily bread. Forgive us our debts, as we also have forgiven our debtors. And lead us not into temptation, but deliver us from the evil one.

Living Surrendered: May your kingdom come, your will be done on earth as it is in heaven.

Circle Prayer

These three kinds of prayer can be viewed as dynamic spheres in which our prayers can be grouped. I call this concept Circle Prayer.

The circle of loving God is where I praise the Lord, worship Him, and adore Him. Then I move to the loving people circle and I begin to pray for the people in my life: my family, my church, people I work with, etc. Then I move into the third circle of living surrendered. Here I surrender my life, my day, my heart to God. So much of prayer is surrendering to God; here is where I make room for that.

In my own life, as I've been praying this pattern of moving through these circles, I find that as I'm praying prayers of surrender, that brings me right back up to loving God and I want to exalt Him again. Surrender leads me to praising and worshiping at a deeper level. Likewise, as I worship Him, it's amazing how often He brings to mind people that I want to know Him, so I begin to pray for people. Praying for people often brings up ways I have acted in self-centeredness in my relationships, which leads to more surrender. There's a natural circular pattern to these three circles of loving God, loving people, and living surrendered.

I have been praying like this for years now, and I have discovered four or five versions of this Circle Prayer. They have really helped me; you might want to try them yourself. You may want to try all of these ways or cycle through them or just settle on one or two that really work for you.

Daily Circle Prayer

In your daily prayer time, try structuring your prayers around these three themes. You can use Circle Prayer as a template, a guide to organize your prayers. For those of you who are more artistic, you might even want to draw three big circles on a page and write in your prayers in each of those circles. At the top of each circle, write in the name of that sphere: Loving God in one, Loving People in another, and Living Surrendered in the third.

Those of you who are more linear, divide a piece of paper into three equal sections (horizontal works better than vertical). Write out your prayers in each category. Whether you write your prayers within the circles, in paragraph form on lined paper, or just pray them out loud, try doing it along these three themes.

Let me give you an example of this. In the Loving God category, spend a couple of minutes just celebrating who God is. Stay in that first circle of Loving God for as long as you want, praising Him, adoring Him, honoring Him. Vocalize His name and characteristics, and praise Him for who He is. Just hang out there for a while. Tell Him what you think of Him.

You've got to keep it real though. There are times in my prayer life when I'm telling God what I think about Him and it's not very happy or pleasant. I'm angry, I'm hurt, I feel deserted. I feel like God is not coming through for me, so I tell Him what I think about Him. That's what prayer is. If you have a problem with that, read the Psalms. They have been used for centuries to teach people how to pray. Jesus prayed the Psalms. Thousands of Christians over the years have prayed the Psalms to God. The point is you're engaging with God. And typically what happens when I'm honest with God is that God lets me vent for a while, and then He lovingly brings me around to seeing who He is and I almost always end up in the surrender circle.

Review the pages above under each section and follow the pattern there. Whenever you feel like it, move to the next circle, Loving People. Spend some time praying for the people in your life or the ones the Holy Spirit prompts you to pray for. If you wish, write their names or a prayer for them. Then in the third circle (or third section of your paper) write down prayers of surrender. In your own words or in the words of Scripture, write prayers of surrender.

Surrender your life to God; surrender your day to Him. Surrender your relationships or troubles you're having. Surrender your finances. Write it down and give it to God. Surrender.

Part of surrendering prayers is examining your heart. Spend a few moments examining your thoughts and motives. Ask the Holy Spirit to reveal things in your life that are not Christlike. As He answers your prayer (and He will!) confess it. Then as you go through that cycle of examining and confessing, you'll want to recommit yourself to God. Living surrendered means recommitting yourself on a regular basis. That's why it's not just onetime surrender but an ongoing basis. After you've been making your requests, stay quiet and listen, and be sensitive to anything the Spirit might want to speak to you.

Centering Circle Prayer

Centering prayer is simply a short prayer to align yourself with God, to re-center your life on God and open yourself to the Holy Spirit. This can be done in a moment or however long you need. I do this all the time. Very simply, I pray: "God, I want to love You. I want to love people. Help me to do that. I surrender to Your love." This can be done anytime and as many times as you want throughout the day and when you retire at night. It helps to recalibrate our hearts to God's heart so we are in sync. I was at a Phil Keaggy concert recently (my favorite musician), and as he was playing he noticed a string that got out of tune, so he just took a second to retune it, to recalibrate the tone of that string to its proper frequency. He didn't stop the whole concert so he could retune, he just did it mid-song, on the fly.

That's what centering prayer does. As we go throughout our day, we will need this kind of tuning frequently. I have great intentions in the morning and then I wander, so I use this as a way to re-center myself in God. The Holy Spirit is the one who will prompt you to pray this, and He will quickly answer. Last night when I went to bed, as I was lying there, I just said to God, "Lord, I want to love You with all my heart, all my soul, all my mind, and all my strength. I want to live my life for You. I want to be about loving people.

Tomorrow may I love people well. So I just surrender to You again tonight."

Meditative Circle Prayer

Circle Prayer can be used as a structure to guide a time of meditative prayer. In an unhurried pace, you can linger on each of the three phrases—loving God, loving people, living surrendered—as long as you want and meditate on them. Meditation is a biblical practice and is extremely valuable as long as you are meditating on biblical truths. This is a time to ponder what these phrases mean in Scripture and how they are reflected in your life. The Holy Spirit can use times like this to shape us, heal us, and work in us His will. Because of the unhurried pace, we are often more attentive and receptive to the work of the Holy Spirit.

Some of the most powerful healing times in our life come during these times of extended focus on God and these biblical truths. Meditating on the love of God is a wonderful healing exercise. Listen to the Holy Spirit. As you're moving through these three circles, listen to His Spirit and respond to His promptings. Perhaps He'll prompt you to look up a scripture and then meditate on that verse. Perhaps He'll reveal attitudes or sin regarding loving people. Perhaps He will show something you need to do or something you need to say to someone. I've never done this without the Holy Spirit showing me an area where I need to re-surrender. These are refreshing, rejuvenating times where I come away charged and energized. As I practice this God deepens me and teaches me. He nourishes me, fills me, enlivens me.

Typically, this takes anywhere from thirty minutes to four hours. Anything longer than that is reserved for a Circle Prayer retreat.

Circle Prayer Retreat

You can structure a whole day or weekend around these three L's and just divide up however much time you'll spend into these three segments of loving God, loving people, and living surrendered. Read Scripture, journal, and write in a notebook as you're meditating. Go for walks. When I take prayer retreats, I love to be outside, so I try to find an area where I can be outside by water or in the woods or even out in a field. I love being outside in God's creation so I'll pray, I'll read, I'll go for a walk, and I'll talk to God about what I just read. I'll think about it deeply and listen attentively.

Circle Prayer Walk

I use Circle Prayer walks to pray in a focused way for people. Prayer-walking is an activity that has been picking up momentum in America for several decades now. As I pray walking through the neighborhood or around our church, I will pray through the three L's. It could be walking around your business or your school. We had a staff member at our church who picked up this practice as a part of coming to work each morning. As he came on our campus, he would drive slowly around, praying these three phrases. I found out about it and thought *how cool is that*? It's a way of encircling our church with prayer. As you are walking and praying, pray that the people in your neighborhood would surrender their lives to God, and pray that your church would grow in loving God and loving people. As you pray through these three L's, don't talk the whole time—listen to the Spirit and let Him guide you as you're praying.

We've covered a lot of ground in this chapter. But the core Christlike characteristic of living in vital connection with God is the foundation and source of all the other Christlike characteristics. As we practice Spiritual Breathing through listening to the voice of the Spirit through the Word of God and then responding back to God in prayer, the Holy Spirit will use this rhythm in our lives to make us more like Christ. As we live in this vital connection, He will be forming our hearts so that we have a heart of worship; that's our next chapter.

Breathing Example

Recently, as I approached a focused time of prayer, I noticed a reluctance in my spirit. I didn't want to pray. I had other things on my mind and at that moment, prayer seemed more like an obstacle or a chore than a privilege. I felt bad about the lack of desire and so I just breathed out a prayer: "Holy Spirit, I confess my lack of desire to pray right now. Breathe into me desire. Breathe into me love for God. Fill me with Your presence. Pray through me. Help me."

Nothing seemed to change so I began to pray a prayer of surrender that started slow and halting and went something like this: "God I just surrender to You . . . As I exhale, I confess apathy and busyness . . . I exhale distraction and independence . . . I confess that my lack of desire to pray is really a statement of my self-centered, independent spirit. Forgive me, Lord. I want to want You. Breathe into me desire. Fill me with passion for You . . . " The next thing I knew, I was pouring out my heart to God, confessing sin and receiving His grace. By the time we were done, it turned out to be an awesome time with God.

Breathing Exercise

The Holy Spirit invites us into an ongoing rhythmic conversation with God. He provides the rhythm as we practice Spiritual Breathing, inhaling His presence and exhaling our sin. As you practice Spiritual Breathing, pay attention to the breathing in and breathing out cycle, using the natural rhythm of your breathing to focus your prayers.

Here is some language to guide our Spiritual Breathing as we live connected to God through prayer:

- As we breathe in, we want to receive the Holy Spirit and say: *"Holy Spirit, breathe in me Your will; I surrender to You."*
- As we breathe out, we want to remove any sin or toxins and say: *"I confess my sin of going my own way and doing my own thing."*
- As we breathe in, we want to receive the Holy Spirit and say: *"Holy Spirit, I receive Your leadership; may Your will be done in my life."*
- As we breathe out, we want to thank God and say: *"Holy Spirit, thank You for Your presence and power."*

Alternate words as we breathe in:
> *"Holy Spirit, breathe in me Your words; help me to pray."*
> *"Holy Spirit, breathe in me desire for You."*
> *"Holy Spirit, breathe in me Your truth; examine my heart."*
> *"Holy Spirit, breathe in me Your life; revive me."*

Alternate words as we breathe out:
> *"I confess my dryness and hardness of heart."*
> *"I confess my busyness."*
> *"I confess my laziness."*
> *"I confess my lack of listening."*

Feel free to add, elaborate, or edit as needed. Remember, the Holy Spirit wants to shape our hearts and minds through prayer as He makes us more like Christ. We just need to learn to *breathe.*

CHAPTER EIGHT

In-Spired Worship

Core Christlike Characteristic: Jesus displayed a heart of worship

The second core Christlike characteristic comes straight from the first. When we "live connected to God," the Holy Spirit produces in us a "heart of worship," a passionate desire to express love and devotion to God with our whole life. When God created us in His image, He designed us to be in intimate relationship with Him where we would breathe in His love and life and then breathe out love back to Him. This response of "loving back" is worship. It goes much, much deeper than what we typically think of when we hear the word worship.

After all that has been written about worship over the years, there is still massive confusion about what worship actually is. It is deeper than music, deeper than church, deeper than symbols, deeper than words; worship is the heart response back to God where we love Him with all of who we are. It comes from the heart but it is expressed with our whole life (Mark 12:30-31). This is the way Jesus lived His life. The vital connection He had with God was not only full of life, it was full of love. He practiced a kind of Spiritual Breathing that maximized life *and* love. Worship is breathing back love to God that comes from the core of who we are. After all, we were not just made to live, we were made to worship.

Recently I ran into a man who was new to our church but whom I hadn't seen in a while. When I commented that I missed him, he surprised me by saying, "I love your church, I just don't like what happens to me when I'm there." Of all the hundreds of conversations I've had about church, this was a new one, and quite honestly one I was rather concerned about. Curious, I asked, "What do you mean?" Out it came: "Whenever I go to your church, I end up crying." This guy was a man's man, an active outdoorsman who could have been an actor for Ford Truck commercials. He was extremely uncomfortable with crying in public but was even more uptight about where the emotions came from. I said, "That's all right, that happens to lots of people." Indeed, he was in a long line of people over the years who've asked me why they end up crying when they come to church: men and women, young and old.

Of course, not everybody cries, but many have felt deeply and profoundly moved. I've had some of them come to me and ask, "What *is* that? What happened?" For some it's during the singing part of the service; for others it's during the preaching part; still others feel it when we pray. They feel something powerful happen, something they can't quite explain, and they want to know "what's up with that?"

Those who are able to articulate their reaction will say they felt this sense of being "inspired"—inspired to do something, inspired to deal with something, inspired to act on something. What is that sense of being inspired, and where does it come from?

I recognize that "feelings" can come from just about anywhere. God has made us emotional beings, and these emotions can be stirred and activated any number of ways. It could be the chord progressions in a song, or the rhythm of drums building to an emotional climax. It could be a story the preacher told or something he said that either consciously or subconsciously reminded you of something that happened that triggered the emotions. It could be that you didn't get enough sleep last night, or the sappy movie you watched is still playing on your heartstrings.

There are plenty of physiological and psychological reasons for why something touches our heart and elicits tears, but there's also a very good spiritual reason, especially when it happens during a time of worship. What these people were experiencing was the presence of the Holy Spirit as He "inspired" them.

Holy Spirit Breathed Worship

Jesus lived a life of inspired worship, and God wants everyone to experience this way of worshiping, spelled more accurately "in-spired worship." A quick trip to the dictionary reveals powerful insights into this word. Webster's says the word "inspire" comes from the Latin, combining *in* and *spirare*, which means "to breathe." We get our English word "spirit" from this word. After giving the etymology, the first definition Webster's offers is "to breathe into."

Just as we discovered back in chapter two, notice the close relationship between these words: spirit and breath.

When we talk about inspired worship then, the meaning is clear: inspired worship is worship that is "in-Spirited," worship that is "breathed into." Inspired worship is worship that is God-breathed, Holy Spirit-breathed.

Of course, many people use the word "inspired" merely to refer to feeling emotionally lifted, but the word is still used regularly to refer to being God-breathed. When we talk about the Bible being inspired, as in the doctrine of inspiration, we are using this word in line with its heritage. The Bible is the God-breathed Scriptures we call the Word of God. Biblical worship, too, is inspired.

As we have seen, breath brings life, so inspired worship is worship where you sense life, or you feel alive; it is life-giving worship. Why? Well, in the strict sense of the word, it is inspired because it is "in-Spirit-ed." The Holy Spirit is breathing His life into the worship. Inspired worship is Christlike worship.

Jesus said God is searching for worshipers who will worship "in spirit and in truth," or rather those who will practice Spiritual Breathing. Just as Spiritual Breathing enables us to live in vital connection with God, so too Spiritual Breathing makes inspired worship possible. In fact, according to Jesus, the only way to worship is to practice Spiritual Breathing.

We have described Spiritual Breathing as an ongoing, rhythmic interaction with God through the Holy Spirit. It involves listening to the Spirit and then responding, inhaling His presence and exhaling our response.

Worship is response, our loving response to God for who He is and what He has done. The response of worship is prompted in the Christian by the Holy Spirit. As we live in vital connection with God, which is the first core Christlike characteristic, the Holy Spirit will form and shape our heart; this is spiritual formation. And the first response in a heart that is living in vital connection with God is the response of worship.

But how exactly does the Spirit do this work in our lives so we can have a heart of worship? To answer that question, we will eavesdrop on a private conversation Jesus had one day with a woman from the region of Samaria, recorded in John 4. In the course of their wide-ranging conversation, Jesus gave some powerful insights about how worship works, what makes worship alive, and what makes it dead. Once I saw some of the dead ways of worshiping, I thought to myself *ouch, I've worshipped that way*. Maybe you have too. The truth is all of us have. Some of us still do.

Confused About Worship

We never learn the name of this woman from Samaria, nor the town she was from. We don't know what she looked like or how old she was. But even without all this knowledge, we know her because she represents each of us, confused about what worship is and thirsting for something more. And just as Jesus engaged with her, so He comes to us too in our confusion, speaks straight to our heart, and brings blinding clarity.

Since we're eavesdropping, we'll join the conversation already in progress. Jesus has just pointed out that she's been looking for love in all the wrong places, and suddenly she decides to change the topic of conversation to something even more controversial: worship.

> *"Sir," the woman said, "I can see that you are a prophet. Our fathers worshiped on this mountain, but you Jews claim that the place where we must worship is in Jerusalem."*
>
> *Jesus declared, "Believe me, woman, a time is coming when you will worship the Father neither on this mountain nor in Jerusalem. You Samaritans worship what you do not know; we worship what we do know, for salvation is from the Jews. Yet a time is coming and has now come when the true worshipers will worship the Father in spirit and truth, for they are the kind of worshipers the Father seeks. God is spirit, and his worshipers must worship in spirit and in truth."*

This is a classic "our way vs. your way" conversation. See the words "our fathers" and "you Jews" in verse 20? In between is the word "but." Classic us vs. them. My way vs. your way. Our way vs. their way. Two different sides. There's a sparring contest, a battle being set up here.

> *"And now, in this corner, all the way from heaven itself, at 6 foot 1 1/2 inches and weighing in at 213 lbs., Jesus the Messiah, the Christ, the Son of the Living God, the 2nd person of the Trinity, the Savior of the Worrrrrrrrld!*
>
> *"And in this corner, from right here in Samaria, at 4 foot 11 and 85 lbs., Sa-mar-i-tan laaaaaaaady!"*
> *Ding, ding, ding!*

Of course, Jesus would never fight somebody about worship. But other people do. Seriously. There's been conflict about worship from the very beginning. What was the first murder in the history of the world? What were they fighting about? Do you know? Worship styles, right? Check it out in Genesis 4:2-9. Cain killed Abel because God liked Abel's worship offering better than his.

Worship is no small issue; it never is. People get all jacked around about the right way to worship. People get really emotional, too emotional, about their preferred way, and the sides are drawn. This could be the Pentecostals vs. the Presbyterians, the Catholics vs. the Protestants, the Baptists vs. the Methodists, the 9:00 service vs. the 11:00, or the NFL vs. Pastor Bill. Most of these controversies are merely preferences; not all of them, but most of them. We each say, "This is just the way I prefer to do it."

If you look at the words this Samaritan lady is using, there's more than preferences. The "you Jews" vs. "we Samaritans" and "your way" vs. "our way" belies deep conflict between two opposing worship styles. See the word "must" in verse 20? This is not merely about preferences, as in "I like green beans, you like corn." When she uses the word "must," immediately she elevates the conversation to "right" vs. "wrong" worship. She even puts these words in the mouth of Jesus: "You Jews claim that we <u>must</u> . . ." I mean, she lays the gauntlet down.

Right vs. Wrong Worship

So it's not just two different views; it's two views that are both claiming to be the right way: this is the way we MUST worship. This word "must" will get used again in a minute, but for now I just want you to see the opposing views here. And what are the two views? Well, on the surface it's the Jews vs. the Samaritans.

Originally the Jews and Samaritans were part of the same Jewish nation, just split at that time into the Northern and Southern Kingdoms. Over time some differences arose between the two, and the Northern Kingdom started doing things that the Southern Kingdom didn't approve of and a rift grew between them. This rift got nasty and full of prejudice to the point where they hated each other. They stopped worshiping together, polarized into different styles of worship, and refused to associate together, even talk to each other; it was bad. They wouldn't even step foot on each others' land. It was the Jewish version of the Hatfields and McCoys.

Now in Jesus' day, there was prejudice and hatred all over the place. Prejudice of men towards women, Jews towards Samaritans, Samaritans towards Jews, Jews towards Gentiles—it was just nasty all over. Jesus, who loves to blow apart dividing walls and prejudice of all kinds, never followed the prejudicial rules. He went right past the barriers of prejudice between Jews and Samaritans, walked across the dividing line right into their space, and struck up a conversation with this Samaritan lady.

But the two views are much deeper than merely Jews vs. Samaritans. These two views cut so much deeper than preferences, deeper than race, deeper than religion. This is a matter of life and death. The real issue is worship that is expired and decaying vs. worship that is in-spired and alive.

Worship That Is Expired and Decaying

Jesus draws some stark contrasts in His conversation with this woman. His message to her in verses 21-23 is that "the kind of worship you are talking about is passing away; it's decaying as we speak." Dead and decaying worship is full of empty and meaningless rituals (and like most things that are decaying, stinks). These rituals cut across labels like Catholic, Baptist, Presbyterian, charismatic, liberal, or evangelical; they can be formal or informal. Outsiders can smell the death, but those who are engaged in it seem to have gotten used to the smell. It's dangerous and toxic to our relationship with God. This kind of worship usually falls into one of two camps. The first kind of expired and decaying worship is worship that is ignorant.

Ignorant Worship. The vast majority of arguments about worship have to do with incidentals and cultural preferences. In our day these incidentals include musical style, instruments, service format, rituals, and clothing. In Jesus' day the incidentals were geographical location, precision of ritual, and ancestral lineage. Jesus says in verses 20-22 that concern about the incidentals of worship misses the point. A revolution of worship is in process and the old, dead worship is passing away. He says if you think worship is about whether it happens on a certain mountain or in the city of Jerusalem, you don't know what worship is all about; your worship is ignorant worship. When we argue about worship styles and instruments, service formats and clothing, it reveals our ignorance of the core issue of worship.

Insincere Worship. The second kind of dead and decaying worship has to do with just going through the motions. God doesn't want our songs, our money, or our church attendance; these are just expressions of what He wants: our heart. Worship is a matter of the heart. One of the passages from the Old Testament that Jesus quoted most was Isaiah 29:13, "These people come near to me with their mouth and honor me with their lips, but their hearts are far from me. Their worship of me is made up only of rules taught by men."

The "rules" Jesus speaks about were the traditions and preferences, or what they called the "right ways" to worship God that were nothing more than cultural trappings. We are in danger of falling into the same trap today. The way most churches worship says more about our cultural preferences than it does about what we really believe about God. Of course, there's nothing wrong with using different cultural expressions, but we must never confuse culture for Christ, style for substance, traditions for truth, or emotion for devotion. Too many Christians see worship as something that only happens on Sunday and they completely miss what God wants. God is looking for a "heart of worship" and wants to see if there is true love, surrender, and obedience as a lifestyle instead of just mouthing words, going through the motions, or looking for a good feeling.

In fact, the first three words of that last sentence reveal something God is actively engaged in: God is looking for a certain kind of worshiper. Jesus responded to this Samaritan woman with the now famous words: "true worshipers will worship the Father in spirit and truth, for they are the kind of worshipers the Father seeks. God is spirit, and his worshipers must worship in spirit and in truth" (John 4:23-24). Jesus is describing for us a Spirit-inspired, Spirit-saturated, Spirit-prompted kind of worship. This is the way He worshipped, and as we become more like Him this kind of worship will characterize our lives as well.

Worship That Is In-Spired and Alive

When Jesus uses the word "must" at the end of verse 24, He not only clarifies the Samaritan woman's misunderstanding but sets the standard for all true worship. As it turns out, there is a right way and a wrong way to worship, but it has nothing to do with the things we argue about.

When God looks for a "heart of worship" what is He looking for? He's looking for worship that is "in spirit and in truth." What exactly does He mean by this? I admit it is a little ambiguous, and there are plenty of opinions about what He meant. For starters, it would be great if we just knew whether or not the word "Spirit" should be capitalized in this verse. You may remember when we were introducing the Holy Spirit in chapter three, we pointed out that the Greek manuscripts in Jesus' day didn't use capital letters the way we do. So scholars argue about whether Jesus is referring to spirit in general or to the Holy Spirit. I say there's no need to argue as both interpretations communicate important truth.

On one level, Jesus is pointing out that worship is a spiritual activity, not a geographical one ("not on this mountain or in Jerusalem"), and since God is Spirit, not confined by space and time, neither is worship. One can worship God anytime, anywhere as long as it is done in spirit and in truth. True worship is a *spirit*ual encounter—our spirit engaged with God's Spirit. It is deeper than location, style, music, or any other forms. This opens up something powerful. If worship is not about time and place, and it's more about spirit and truth than about location and style, it means we can worship anywhere, anytime. Not only can we, but we should. We're talking 24/7 worship. Worship is a lifestyle. Not singing 24/7 but an attitude of worship where the deepest parts of who we are, our spirit, is in connection and communion with God.

On another level, Jesus is also talking about the Holy Spirit. When we talk about God's Spirit, we are talking about the Holy Spirit. Later in John's Gospel, Jesus uses these two words Spirit and truth together again. Jesus, speaking of the Holy Spirit, told His disciples in John 16:13 that "when he, the Spirit of truth, comes, he will guide you into all truth." The Spirit guides us into understanding and worship that is based on truth. He does this by inspiring, illuminating, and interpreting.

The Spirit inspires attraction and desire for God.

Why do we feel drawn to God? The Bible says repeatedly that no one seeks God, and yet we feel drawn to Him. How can this be? The only reason we seek God is because the Spirit is working in us to draw us to Him; He is breathing into us desire for God. Apart from the inspiring work of the Spirit we would not pursue God. Why do we desire to lift our hands, to voice our praise, to offer ourselves, to kneel, to cry, to surrender? These are all actions inspired by the Holy Spirit. They don't just come from random feelings, the Holy Spirit breathes them into us, and as we've seen, this action of "breathing into" is the in-Spiring work of the Spirit. Part of this in-Spiration comes from how the Holy Spirit illuminates the nature and character of God.

The Spirit illuminates the nature and character of God.

In addition to worshiping "in Spirit," Jesus said we must worship "in truth." Our worship of God must be shaped by an accurate understanding of who God is. Ignorant worship leads to idolatrous worship. Since the Holy Spirit is the "Spirit of truth," He can be trusted to guide us into biblical worship. Without the illuminating work of the Spirit, we end up with caricatures of God ranging from an angry judge waiting to pounce on our every mistake to a harmless, benevolent domesticated god to a cosmic genie who waits to grant our every selfish desire.

Our conception of God is the most important thing about us and a predictor of how we will navigate life. All of our problems in life can be traced back to an inaccurate conception of God. Likewise, an accurate conception of God provokes deeper trust, greater love, and a resilient hope, no matter how hard life gets. Only a man who believes Job 32:8 and 33:4 can say what he says in Job 13:15. (Guess you're going to have to look them up!)

The Spirit interprets the words and actions of God.

As the Holy Spirit illuminates the true nature and character of God, He guides us to worship in truth, and this worship deepens our knowledge of and intimacy with Him. Admittedly, God's words and actions aren't always easy to understand. That's why the Holy Spirit also acts as an interpreter on our behalf, helping us understand, as Paul points out in 1 Corinthians 2:12,14: "We have not received the spirit of the world but the Spirit who is from God, *that we may understand* what God has freely given us" (italics mine).

Just as the Holy Spirit inspired, illuminates, and helps interpret the Word of God for us, so He inspires us and illuminates and interprets God's actions for us so that we, with increasing understanding, can worship God in Spirit and in truth.

With increased knowledge comes deeper love which prompts heartfelt worship. Knowing God intimately leads to loving God deeply. Along the way, as the Spirit illuminates God's character, He will also illuminate ours. As He searches our heart, when He finds sin He will point it out to us. As He exposes the holy nature of God, that same light will expose sin in us. That is why throughout the Bible whenever you find intimacy in worship it is often linked with confession (e.g. Isaiah 6:1-7). As the Holy Spirit breathes into us and forms a heart of worship in us, that process includes cleansing and purifying our hearts.

Just as Spiritual Breathing enables us to live in vital connection with God, so too Spiritual Breathing makes inspired worship possible. Authentic worship has a rhythm to it that mirrors Spiritual Breathing. Worship in Spirit and in truth is the rhythm of the Spirit revealing God to us and our response according to that revelation. The rhythmic interaction of worship involves listening to the Spirit and then responding, inhaling His presence and exhaling our response, breathing in His holiness and breathing out our sin. Worship in Spirit and in truth is an essential part of the Holy Spirit's ongoing work to make us more and more like Christ.

Breathing Example

The first Sunday night of each month we have a service of prayer and worship at our church called (surprise) First Sunday. I was leading one particular night and had just finished a song but kept softly playing my guitar as I looked out over the crowd, listening for the leading of the Holy Spirit. I sensed the Holy Spirit prompting me to say that there were some that night struggling with fear. So I voiced what I was sensing and invited people to simply exhale their fear and breathe in the love and presence of God. Later I heard multiple people share how they were struggling with fear and how God met them that night. As people gathered around them and prayed for them, God breathed love and power into them, filling them with His presence. Tears flowed, smiles broke out and when we began to sing again, the sense of the presence of God was so profound, no one wanted to leave.

Breathing Exercise

We were made to worship, and the Holy Spirit wants to breathe into us His Spiritual Oxygen and form in us a heart of worship. As we enter into the rhythm of Spiritual Breathing, the Holy Spirit will shape our response. We just need to keep breathing. As you practice Spiritual Breathing, pay attention to the breathing in and breathing out cycle, using the natural rhythm of your breathing to focus your prayers.

Here is some language to guide your Spiritual Breathing as the Spirit forms in you a heart of worship:

- As we breathe in, we want to receive the Holy Spirit and say: *"Holy Spirit, breathe in me the truth of the character of God and correct my caricatures of who You are."*
- As we breathe out, we want to remove any sin or toxins and say: *"I confess my sin, as well as my false perceptions of who You are."*
- As we breathe in, we want to receive the Holy Spirit and say: *"Holy Spirit, I receive Your presence. Breathe in me Your love."*
- As we breathe out, we want to thank God and say: *"Holy Spirit, thank You for Your presence and power."*

Alternate words as we breathe in:
> *"Holy Spirit, breathe in me Your holiness . . . "*
> *"Holy Spirit, breathe in me truth . . . "*
> *"Holy Spirit, breathe in me knowledge of God . . . "*

> *"Holy Spirit, breathe in me revelation and insight… "*

Alternate words as we breathe out:

> *"I confess my attempts to make You more like me… "*
> *"I confess my trying to domesticate you… "*
> *"I confess my idolatry…"*
> *"I confess my rebellion and independence…"*

Feel free to add, elaborate, or edit as needed. Remember, the Holy Spirit wants to shape our hearts and minds through worship as He makes us more like Christ. We just need to learn to *breathe.*

SECTION THREE

. . . .

Loving People

· ·

CHAPTER NINE

Loving Like Christ

Core Christlike Characteristic: Jesus related with other-centered love

O f the six core Christlike characteristics, this third one, the way we relate to people, is the most public and visible. The way we relate to people is the most noticeable and enduring thing about each of us; it is how we will be known by others. You might call it our "relational aroma." Like our own breath, other people tend to notice it before we do.

Everybody has a certain "air" about them, how others perceive them as they relate to the people around them. This is our relational aroma. Furthermore, like our breath, our relational aroma is determined by internal issues. What comes out of us is a reflection of what is going on inside of us. The interior life always produces the exterior life. That is why we said earlier that the first core Christlike characteristic, living "connected to God through the Word and prayer," produces all the other characteristics. As we live "connected to God," the Holy Spirit forms and develops in us a heart of love for God and other people.

The vital connection Jesus had with God the Father formed in Him a love for people that characterized His ministry from beginning to end. Without question, the most compelling characteristic of Jesus' life was the way He loved. No one loved like Jesus. As we study His life in the Gospels, love shows up again and again.

Matthew, Mark, and Luke all record the inauguration of Jesus' ministry with a Trinitarian reunion of sorts, as the Holy Spirit rests on Jesus and God the Father says, "You are my son, whom I love" (Mark 1:11). Grounded in that love, Jesus embarked on a ministry of loving others. Luke pictures Jesus immediately leaving that scene with the Father's love ringing in His ears, being "filled with" and "led by the Holy Spirit," the evidence of which is love (Galatians 5:14, 18, 22.) The first extended account of Jesus' teaching in Matthew (Sermon on the Mount) records Him sounding the theme of love again and again. John says that Jesus came because of love and to reveal God's heart of love (John 3:16, 1:18, 17:23). When Jesus was asked which is the greatest commandment, out of 613 different Old Testament commands, He summarized them all with "love God and love people" (Mark 12:30-31).

To encounter Jesus of Nazareth was to encounter the love of God. Jesus loved with unconditional acceptance and piercing honesty. Love motivated Him to leave heaven and come to earth, and love drove Him to complete His mission on the cross. His teaching captured the imagination of the masses, but it was His love that marked every personal encounter.

When John wants to describe how Jesus related to the disciples, love is his summary (John 13:1). When Jesus encounters a woman caught in sin, His love is protective and forgiving towards the woman while at the same time infuriating and convicting the Pharisees (John 8:3-11). As He's being rejected by the Rich Young Ruler, Mark pauses to tell us, "Jesus looked at him and loved him" (Mark 10:21).

His way of loving stood out so much that when He needed to name the one characteristic that would unmistakably identify people as *His* disciples, He said it would be their love for those around them (John 13:34). Love is the litmus test of whether we are really disciples becoming like Jesus or merely religious moralists using Jesus for our own purposes.

Jesus' love was pure and powerful but kind and tender. Unpredictable without being capricious, He made people feel exposed and safe at the same time. His love was active and compassionate, combining a strong gentleness with fierce holiness that kept people surprised and marveling. To a world living in a desert of self-centeredness and oppression, Jesus' way of relating was a refreshing rain shower on parched, dry souls.

I have a brother who lived in Afghanistan for 18 years. Tim knows what brutal, oppressive heat is like. He's talked about times when it's 125 degrees and the heat is suffocating, but you still wrap yourself with garments because the hot wind and sand literally rip into your skin, sandblasting you. He said it's like being in a blast furnace; you can't even imagine the heat. Then he wants me to come visit him!

A couple of years ago he came and visited our family during one of our hot spells in Ohio. One afternoon, while Tim and his family were out for a bike ride, we had one of those quick rainstorms that blow up in Cleveland. My wife and I were concerned as the sky turned dark and menacing, and sure enough torrents of rain began pouring down. We stood in the garage waiting for them to return from the bike ride, and when we saw them it seemed they were riding their bikes way too slowly for being out in the pouring rain. As they got closer, we noticed Tim's face: grinning ear to ear, water running down his face and beard, he was almost giddy. He got off the bike, stretched out his arms, and turned his face toward the sky, drinking up the heavenly liquid with every pore of his body. Next thing I knew, both of our families were out on the driveway dancing and splashing in the downpour. Adults became children as we all reveled in the saturating, refreshing rain shower.

Being around Jesus of Nazareth was like experiencing a gentle rain in the hot desert. He brought the refreshing showers of His joyful love everywhere He went. As Jesus walked throughout the streets and villages of Israel, He showered the people with His love. And as He loved, people got a taste of the love of God. It made such an impact on the apostle John that his writings are saturated with the language and description of this kind of love. He is sometimes referred to as the "Apostle of Love," and the fourth chapter of his first letter is the real "love chapter" of the New Testament. He uses the word "love" twenty-seven times in this chapter alone, three times as many as Paul does in 1 Corinthians 13. But it's not the number of times he uses the word that is so noteworthy, it's what he says about love and how we can love like Jesus that is so important.

Love That Comes from God

Right after John calls us to love one another in verse 7, he explains what kind of love we are to love with: the love that "comes from God." This is the most important truth about love that Jesus came to demonstrate: we are to love with God's love. When we love with our love, our self-centeredness ruins the loving and it becomes damaging and destructive.

Jesus wasn't the first person on planet earth to love; He was just the only one who gave us the pure expression of God's kind of love. This was the secret to His loving: He loved with God's love.

Everyone loves, but most love is self-centered love. Jesus came to give us a taste of God's love. It's worth exploring this kind of love for a moment. The better we understand the nature of the love Jesus modeled, the better we will be at cooperating with the Spirit and loving like Christ.

This language in verse 7, "love comes from God," is where we will start. John says "love comes from God" because "God is love" (v. 8). Love is not just an attribute or characteristic of God, it is His very nature. This simple three-word sentence, "God is love," means God's essence is love. God loves like the sun shines. He emanates love.

God the Father Emanates Love

For all eternity God has been emanating love. That means *before our world existed, love existed.* Since eternity past God has been loving. But love is not an abstract concept;

for love to exist there must be relationship. There must be one who loves and one who is loved.

That begs the question: who was God loving before He created the world? The answer is hinted at in the very next verse, verse 9: "This is how God showed his love among us: He sent his one and only Son into the world." This verse expands our view into the nature of God, a view that is completed just a few verses later: "He has given us of his Spirit. And we have seen and testify that the Father has sent his Son to be the Savior of the world" (1 John 4:13-14). Notice the language in these verses: Spirit, Father, Son. Not only is God love, but this love is a Trinitarian love.

Before our world existed, in eternity past, intimate love was flowing between God the Father, God the Son, and God the Holy Spirit. John is telling us that love comes from the eternal, Trinitarian God and to love like God is to learn to love like the Trinity loves. God's love is first and foremost how God the Father loves the Son and the Holy Spirit and how the Spirit and Son love the Father and each other. Because this love is so pure, Trinitarian love is the model for all healthy relating. It's worth noting that there's never been a fight between the members of the Trinity.

We get a beautiful picture of this love in Luke 3:22 at the beginning of Jesus' ministry: "The Holy Spirit descended on him in bodily form like a dove. And a voice came from heaven: 'You are my Son, whom I love.'" There's Jesus, the incarnate second Person of the Trinity, standing in the river, and the Holy Spirit descends on Him in the form of a dove and then a voice. Who is the voice? Well, you can tell in the next phrase when He says "you are my Son." So the voice is obviously the voice of the Father. It's an amazing picture: the eternal, transcendent God as Father, Son, and Spirit condescends to take on temporary, earthly attributes in the form of a voice, a man, and a dove! And of all the things He could have said, He says "I love you." So simple. So powerful.

Ever wonder why we get the dove? Why isn't it enough to have just the voice of the Father? After all, the Holy Spirit never says anything in this scene. I think it's because when God loves, He loves as a Trinity. The Father, Son, and Holy Spirit have had this love fest going on for all eternity. Maybe that's why the most often repeated phrase in the Bible is "His love endures forever." The most pure and powerful love of all is God's love, which is why Trinitarian love is the model for all healthy relating. When we love people with God's love, it heals and restores and nourishes. God's love is the most powerful force in the universe. God's love can resurrect a dead marriage and give life to relationships broken by sin. Remember this: there's hope for any relationship when we love with God's kind of love.

But to say I am supposed to love with Trinitarian love feels really ethereal and out there. Let's put this in terms we can get a handle on. God the Father isn't seen expressing love to Himself, Jesus the Son isn't seen bragging about Himself, and the Holy Spirit is the shyest of them all; the love between the Trinity is radical *other-centeredness*. Each of the members of the Trinity focuses on each other, not themselves.

This brings us to a powerful truth: *the essence of Trinitarian love is other-centeredness.* This simply means that love is doing that which has the other person's best interests in mind. I am focused on what the other person wants and needs, not on what I want and think I need. Other-centered love is the exact opposite of self-centered love, which by the way is a great definition for sin. Sin is self-centeredness. God's love is other-centeredness.

Back to 1 John 4, John says that we are to love with God's love and that God is love; He emanates other-centered love. But even as helpful as it is to understand that God's love is other-centered love, it's still a little ethereal. We wonder what exactly does that look like in my life. And that's what John wants us to hear next: verse 9, "this is how God showed his love among us. He sent his one and only son into the world that we might live through him." What's he talking about?

God the Son Embodies Love

He's talking about what we call the incarnation. It's a theological word we all should know. Incarnate means "in flesh, or embody." It's the idea of God the Father, who **emanates** love, sending God the Son to the earth, who **embodies** love by becoming flesh. Jesus is the embodiment of the love of God so you can feel the love of God in a hug. You can see the love of God through eyes. God's love becomes tangible, touchable. God takes His love that's emanating from the heavens and brings it on this planet and fills a human body. This is what Christmas is all about. God became flesh, one of us; His name was Jesus of Nazareth. Jesus came to show us what God's love looks like in everyday life. He came to reveal God's love, to explain it to us in ways we can grasp.

Because Jesus lived a life of love, it made perfect sense to the disciples when He turned to them at the Last Supper and said, "Love one another. As I have loved you, so you must love one another" (John 13:34). Jesus makes it clear that He is talking about a certain kind of love. He wants them to love the way He did, with Christlike love, or other-centered love. God's Love = Trinitarian Love = Christlike Love = Other-Centered Love.

In the Image of God

Actually, we were all designed to love like Christ; that was the original plan. Back in Genesis 1, notice the Trinitarian language and the original plan God has for humanity: "Then God said, 'Let us make man in our image, in our likeness' . . . So God created man in his own image, in the image of God he created him; male and female he created them" (Genesis 1:26a-27). God, who is love, made us in His image. Being made in the image of God reveals three very important truths about each one of us. Being made in the image of God defines who I am.

1. Defines Who I Am

My identity is grounded in the fact that I was made in the image of God. The first word about each of us, before talk of personality or looks or abilities, is that each person is made in the image of God. The word "likeness/image" means to "reflect something else, to represent something else." So to be made in the image of God means that:

- I was made to reflect God on this earth
- I was made to represent God on this earth.

How do I reflect and represent God on this earth? By the way I relate. So we say,

- I was made to relate with God and others.

We were not placed on this earth to amass wealth, achieve accomplishments, or seek comfort. To put it concisely, *we were made to relate with others in a way that reflects and represents God.*

The second truth we can draw from being made in the image of God is that it determines how we value others and ourselves.

2. Determines How I Value

A coin is not assigned value by the worth of the precious metal it's made of but by the image stamped on it. Neither is the value of a person determined by their race or social position or abilities but by the image stamped on their soul. Each person is made in the image of God; therefore each person is of infinite value. My value and the value of every person I meet is grounded in the fact that each of us was made in the image of God. Therefore it matters greatly how I relate to each person. And since I was made to relate with others in a way that reflects and represents God, being made in the image of God *directs* how I relate to other people.

3. Directs How I Relate

We have already seen that the essence of God is love, so to be made in the image of God means I was made to love others with God's love. I am to relate to people with the love of God.

Once we identify these three overarching truths, it's pretty easy to see how Jesus embodied each of these and how they drove the way Jesus loved. Grounded in the security of being loved by the Father, He launched out into a life of loving, treating each person as if they were of infinite value and relating to them with this radical other-centered way of loving. No wonder people were drawn to Him! And no wonder that each of His disciples who wrote in the New Testament spoke again and again about His love.

This was God's original plan for each of us: that we love with His love. To make it crystal clear for us, He sent us Jesus to embody and illustrate this way of loving. So when Jesus said to His disciples "As I have loved you, so you must love one another," He was seeking to restore God's original vision for why we were made. But what exactly did the disciples think when Jesus said "love as I have loved"? More specifically, in practical terms, what does Christlike love look like?

The Gospels record scene after scene of Jesus accepting the rejected, forgiving the sinner, healing the broken, listening to the forgotten, and including the outcast. We see how Jesus acts, hear what He says, and watch where He goes. But it may be Paul in the Epistles who gives us the most succinct and helpful summary of what Christlike love looks like. In fact, echoing these same words of Jesus in John 13:34, Paul says in Ephesians 5:2 that we are to "Live a life of love, just as Christ loved us and gave himself up for us as a fragrant offering and sacrifice to God."

Loving Like Jesus

Paul does not leave it up to his readers to insert their own definition of how to love people; he calls us to love people "just as Christ loved us." This verse contains two primary, powerful ideas that reveal how Christ loved us. The first is seen in the very next words that come after "Christ loved us." Paul says He "gave himself . . . as an offering."

1. **Giving/Offering Love**
   a. **Offer Yourself**

You can give without loving, but you cannot love without giving. Christ's love is a giving kind of love. The most famous verse in the Bible, John 3:16, ties these two ideas together as well as any other place in the Bible: "God so loved the world that he gave . . . " Paul calls this kind of loving love that gives "a fragrant offering to God." I like how the NLT translates Ephesians 5:2: "Live a life filled with love, following the example of Christ. He loved us and offered himself as a sacrifice for us." The phrase "He loved us and offered himself" is especially poignant.

"Love offers" is not language we typically use, but it is biblical language and is very helpful to describe what Christlike love looks like. The "offering" nature of this love describes a core characteristic of Christlike love. To "offer" is to present something for acceptance: to attempt to give somebody something that may be taken or refused, usually something desirable. Christlike love is not forced on someone; it is offered, given, presented. It may be accepted or rejected.

This is why true love is vulnerable; it involves risk. Many people withhold love because of the fear of being rejected; it's risky, and we may get hurt. The fact of the matter is if you love you *will* get hurt. Christ did; you will too. Christlike love is by nature a vulnerable love. The amazing thing is that knowing full well He would be rejected, even crucified, Jesus held nothing back; He offered His love to any and all who would receive Him.

There are two ways that we practice this "offering love" that are more important than any other. These are key secrets to Christlike loving, and they will revolutionize any relationship.

1. Notice specifically what Ephesians 5:2 says Christ offered: He offered "himself."

Christlike love is self-giving love. Self-giving love involves revealing who I am, and *revelation is always the pathway to intimacy*. Out of fear of being rejected, many people stay on the surface in their loving and don't reveal the deeper parts of their heart. If they do give, they give physical, material gifts. There's nothing wrong with this kind of giving, it's just not enough; it's shallow, surface loving. Offering self-giving love to someone means we give of what we have and, more importantly, who we are.

Self-giving love gives someone access to our heart and reveals those places in our heart where hopes and dreams and fears and insecurities dwell. It's loving with transparency, the real you. This kind of loving has the aroma of authenticity to it. It's the difference between eating a TV dinner vs. a homemade meal, or hearing someone describe how good a particular dish was vs. actually tasting it yourself. When we love well, when we love like Christ, we are giving someone a taste of God's love.

Self-giving love is sacrificial love. Jesus didn't offer gold and silver, physical treasures, He offered *Himself.* Explaining this to His disciples, He said, "Greater love has no one than this, that he lay down his life for his friends" (John 15:13).

2. The second way of offering Christlike love is to offer grace to the person you are in relationship with. Paul says in Colossians 4:6, "Let your conversation be always full of grace." You could call this "conversational grace" or, what I prefer, "relational grace." We are loving people when our conversation and responses are full of grace. What does this look like? Ephesians 4:32 is helpful: "Be kind and compassionate to one another, forgiving each other, just as in Christ God forgave you." Relational grace is extending kindness, gentleness, patience, and forgiveness to others. It is making allowance for people's faults. It is being compassionate and forgiving to those we are in relationship with.

A number of years ago, my wife and I had one of those little spats that comes out of nowhere and quickly escalates. Ever been there? This one was a doozy and turned hurtful. We both said some things that hurt the other, and to my shame Andrea was the first one to take a step towards reconciliation. I have no idea what we were arguing about, but I will never forget what happened next. As we were standing there in the kitchen, she took a step towards me and, holding out her arms, said, "Will you forgive me?" I stood there with my hands in my pockets, still mad but now even more hacked because she was being more Christlike than I and said, "Of course, yes, I forgive you." She hugged me just as I was and then uttered one of the greatest lines in the history of relationships: "How can you forgive me with your hands in your pockets?" At that point I lost it and broke down in shameful crying as we hugged, extending and enjoying real forgiveness to and with each other.

Here's a helpful contrast to remember: self-centered love is focused on what I can *get from* others; Christlike love is focused on what I can *give to* others.

Back to Ephesians 5:2, when Paul says "Christ loved us and gave himself up *for* us" the word "for" means "on behalf of" or "for the sake of." It indicates movement, an action toward another person, on behalf of that person. Of course, love is a verb and so loving entails movement. The picture here is that Christ's love moves out toward other people, like walking toward someone with your arms open to give them a hug.

Self-centered love   vs.   Other-centered love

Love always has movement and focus. It is either moving in or moving out. It is either focused on self or focused on another. Christ's love is focused, moving toward others. This is the second picture of Christlike love:

2. Other-Centered Love
b. Offer Grace

It should be no surprise that we see Jesus practicing other-centered love since we saw that other-centered love is Trinitarian love and Jesus is the second Person of the Trinity. He moved toward us, reached out to us when He left heaven and came to earth. The Gospels record page after page of Jesus reaching out to people, moving toward people to love them. Jesus truly lived His life "for" others. His death was "for the sake of" others.

The Greek language has a special word for the kind of love that is reaching out, extending out, focused out toward others: *agape* love. All the instances of love in 1 John that we looked at above were this Greek word *agape*. Other-centered love is the core definition of God's kind of love. It is the most accurate reflection of God that we are capable of on this earth. And remember, since we have been made in the image of God, our purpose in this world is to accurately reflect and represent God by the way we relate to others. We do this when, like Christ, we love with other-centered love.

It's hard to overstate the stark contrast between self-centered love and other-centered love. Every relationship we're in is damaged by self-centered loving. Every relationship problem can be traced back to one or both people practicing self-centered loving. But the opposite is also true: every relationship can be improved by other-centered loving. No matter how bad a relationship is, it can get better when we learn to practice Christlike, other-centered loving.

Jesus came to show us how to love, and the night before He died He *commanded* the disciples to love one another just as He loved them. Later that night He introduced to them the One who would give them the ability to love just as He did: the Holy Spirit.

Jesus knew that His disciples were not going to be able to love if they tried to love in their own strength. And so He said "there's One coming, the Holy Spirit, who will *empower* you to love with the love of God." God the Father emanates love, God the Son embodies love, and God the Holy Spirit empowers love.

God the Holy Spirit Empowers Love

Loving with Trinitarian, other-centered love is not something one does by trying harder. You cannot love people the way they need to be loved in your own strength. You must be empowered by the Holy Spirit or you will end up "loving" with your own self-centered, destructive ways, not even aware that you are doing far more damage than good.

The Bible uses multiple images to communicate how God empowers us to love. One of my favorite is in Ephesians 3 where Paul prays for people to receive this power. As you read these verses, watch how he connects the Holy Spirit, love, and power all together: "I pray that out of his glorious riches he may strengthen you with power through his Spirit in your inner being, so that Christ may dwell in your hearts through faith. And I pray that you, being rooted and established in love, may have power, together with all the saints, to grasp how wide and long and high and deep is the love of Christ, and to know this love that surpasses knowledge—that you may be filled to the measure of all the fullness of God" (Ephesians 3:16-19).

Paul knows that what people need most to live the Christian life is the empowering of the Holy Spirit. He knows that at the very deepest part of who we are (our "inner being") we must be rooted and established in God's love. He knows that we need to have Christ formed in us, living in us. So he prays that the Holy Spirit may empower us in our inner being, knowing that this empowering work of the Spirit will establish us and root us in God's love.

Most of our self-centered, damaging ways of "loving" others comes out of a lack of being "rooted and established" in the secure, eternal love of God. Without this security, we waver between using people and needing people, looking to them to meet our needs for security and significance. Only the Holy Spirit, who fills us with the love of Christ, can enable us to love people the way they need to be loved and in a way that is healthy for both them and us.

When we love people with our selfish love we end up wounding and damaging them. But when we love with God's love, it heals and restores and nourishes. I've seen God's love resurrect a dead marriage and give life to relationships damaged by sin. I've seen people learn to breathe in the Spiritual Oxygen of God and, empowered with that love, turn barren, dead relationships into flourishing, life-giving ones. We desperately need this kind of love in relationships today! As we said earlier, there's hope for any relationship when we love with God's kind of love.

Think of the typical interactions you have with people throughout the day. We can pause before and even during these interactions and in a breath ask the Holy Spirit to fill us with God's love. Though there certainly are plenty of scenarios where interacting with our spouse, children, friend, or coworker is spontaneous and unexpected, there are also many predictable times when we can practice Spiritual Breathing to help us love like Christ.

When you come home from work, tired and exhausted, pause in the car for twenty seconds before you get out and do some Spiritual Breathing. Breathe out your frustrations, disappointments, anger, and high-strung emotions, and breathe in God's love, grace, patience, and presence. In fact, you can do this every time you get out of the car. Before you have to make a difficult phone call, pause and breathe:

inhale God's presence, exhale your tension and anxiety. A little bit of practice and this becomes second nature to us. Once we get good at it, we can steal a breath of God's love in the most unassuming places and in a surprisingly brief amount of time.

When we get hurt in a relationship, we can learn to practice Spiritual Breathing and exhale the hurt and inhale God's love and grace. When we are disappointed or let down, we can exhale the disappointment and inhale God's truth that He is sovereignly working all things out for our good and His glory. When we sense anger rising, we can breathe in His gentleness and breathe out our irritation. When conflict is escalating, we can breathe in God's loving patience and ask Him to fill us with the ability to see from the other person's viewpoint.

Our relationships can be revolutionized by this simple practice of Spiritual Breathing. We can bring the refreshing love of God into the relationships we are involved in. We can learn to love those around us with God's love and in so doing become more like Christ.

Breathing Example

I had just finished preaching and was greeting some people and praying for others between services when a man came up to me. He was angry. At me. As he expressed himself, I found myself wanting to interrupt and offer a defense against what I felt were groundless accusations that had been birthed in destructive gossip. In the quietness of my heart, I breathed out a quick prayer asking the Holy

Spirit to breathe into me God's love. As I listened to this man vent, I felt compassion for him. I wondered what had happened to make him so unforgiving, so judgmental, and so disrespectful. God filled me with the ability to love this man and instead of an escalating heated exchange, we had a calm discussion and he ended up walking away with a new perspective. Spiritual Breathing enabled me to respond with grace and love instead of reacting with anger.

Breathing Exercise

Loving people requires a steady supply of Spiritual Oxygen. We must breathe in and receive His love and breathe out relational toxins that damage our relationships. As you practice Spiritual Breathing, pay attention to the breathing in and breathing out cycle, using the natural rhythm of your breathing to focus your prayers.

Here is some language to guide our Spiritual Breathing as we seek to love others:

- As we breathe in, we want to receive the Holy Spirit and say: *"Holy Spirit, breathe in me Your love; fill me with Your love."*
- As we breathe out, we want to remove any sin or toxins and say: *"I confess my self-centeredness and pride."*
- As we breathe in, we want to receive the Holy Spirit and say: *"Holy Spirit, I receive Your love; I open my heart to receive Your love."*

- As we breathe out, we want to thank God and say: *"Holy Spirit, thank You for Your presence and power."*

Alternate words as we breathe in:
> *"Holy Spirit, breathe in me forgiveness."*
> *"Holy Spirit, breathe in me patience and a listening ear."*
> *"Holy Spirit, breathe in me the compassion of Jesus."*
> *"Holy Spirit, breathe in me courage to love."*

Alternate words as we breathe out:
> *"I confess my hurts and wounds."*
> *"I confess my lack of love."*
> *"I confess my narcissism."*
> *"I confess my insecurities."*

Feel free to add, elaborate, or edit as needed. Remember, the Holy Spirit wants to shape our hearts and minds through loving people as He makes us more like Christ. We just need to learn to *breathe.*

· ·

CHAPTER TEN

Loving People to Christ

Core Christlike Characteristic: Jesus intentionally sought out people to show and share the Good News

Several years after I was born, my parents met a woman named Onnalee Kaufman who would change our family forever. One of the meanings of the name Onnalee is "light" and she began to shine her light into the darkness of our home. My parents weren't Christians at the time even though they were good, moral American people attending church. Because they were such good people, the fact that both of them were living in darkness and headed towards hell wasn't immediately obvious. They were both raised in good, religious homes and went to church every week: my dad was a Lutheran and my mom was a Methodist. Instead of having kids who were Lutherdists, they had kids who were as lost as they were.

That's when Onnalee came into our life. She and her husband Bob sought out my parents and began to build a relationship with them. She invited us to their house for meals and walks on their vast property. After about a year of friendship, they invited my parents to a Bible study on the Gospel of Mark. During the study of Mark, my parents became aware that they did not have a personal relationship with Jesus. Bob and Onnalee shared with them the Good News of Jesus Christ and the need to surrender their lives to Him as their personal Savior.

Eventually, both my parents accepted Christ and began following Him. Then Onnalee began to work on my sister and me. Using a wordless book of colored pages, Onnalee presented the gospel to me as a five-year-old. I understood enough to invite Christ into my life and began my journey as a Christian under her tutelage.

As I sit here writing this, I wonder what might have happened if Onnalee hadn't *intentionally* sought out my parents and shared the Good News of Christ with them. What might have happened if she hadn't shared the gospel with *me*? My life and future was eternally affected by her intentional evangelism. I am forever grateful for her loving, evangelistic efforts.

The odd thing about this story is that both of my parents were heavily involved in churches growing up. They were surrounded by good, moral, church-going people, some of them no doubt Christians. But no one had ever shared with them the need or how to personally trust Christ as their Savior.

Opting Out of Evangelism

Unfortunately, many Christians and the churches they attend have adopted a version of Christianity that leaves evangelism to the evangelists and preachers. Even in so-called evangelical circles, evangelism is often left to those with the gift of evangelism. Discipleship is narrowly defined as praying, reading the Bible, and having devotions. But discipleship without evangelism is not biblical discipleship. You can't become like Christ if you're not doing intentional evangelism. Or, to put it another way, you can't become like Christ if you're not a part of bringing people to Christ. Intentional Evangelism is a Core Christlike Characteristic. Yet this characteristic is an area in which most disciples, oxymoronically, are notoriously weak.

To restore a more holistic, biblical discipleship and help people identify where they are in their growth toward Christlikeness, I developed a tool called the Next Step Survey. (If you'd like to take the survey go to http://opendoor.tv/nextstep/.) When we first rolled this out in our church, person after person told me that taking the survey confirmed what they already knew: they were very weak in evangelism.

And yet, even though they had known they were weak in evangelism, they were doing nothing about it. They reasoned with themselves, "I'm really strong in two or three of the core Christlike characteristics, and that balances out how weak I am in this one. After all, nobody can be strong in everything." That kind of thinking works if becoming like Christ is like being a renaissance man, but it's not. Christian maturity is *not* an attempt to be a well-rounded person; it's the adventure of becoming *like* Christ. Paul said in Ephesians 4:13 we are to grow up into "the whole measure of the fullness of Christ." One can't say, "Well, I'm Christlike in this area, but not in this, and that's okay."

If we are growing to be more like Christ, it is because of progress in each area of the core Christlike characteristics.

To ignore or explain away an area of weakness is like saying a baseball player can excel in hitting and catching the ball but can't throw it. Throwing the ball is a core skill that every baseball player must learn. For sure, some will throw the ball better than others, but it's not a skill you can skip and still expect to be considered a baseball player.

If we are serious about becoming like Christ, we must be "growing in every way more and more like Christ" (Ephesians 4:15 NLT); we can't pick and choose which areas we wish to skip. And yet that is exactly what many people do when it comes to evangelism. We say things like "it's not my gift" or "I'm not a salesman" or "I'm not a pastor."

Part of the reason for our failure in evangelism is because of how we have represented it. We've turned evangelism into memorizing a sales pitch, delivering it, and then "closing the deal." Jesus would be turned off by our approach. What we need is to be reacquainted with Christlike evangelism and discipleship—evangelism and discipleship as practiced by Jesus.

Christlike Evangelism

No person has ever lived with more intentionality than Jesus Christ. And there's never been a person whose intention was more focused on people than Jesus. He was driven by a mission that in His own words was to "seek and save the lost" (Luke 19:10). Jesus intentionally sought out people to show and share the Good News of God's love wherever He went. Regardless of a person's economic standing, social status, or current lifestyle, Jesus' love for people motivated Him to reach out to them.

Though the Gospels record much of the teaching of Jesus, they are also laced with the stories of many of the people He touched. Consider this representative list: fishermen, tax collectors, grieving mothers, desperate fathers, adulterers, religious leaders, Roman soldiers, the blind and deaf, the demon-possessed, little children, the lame, lepers, aristocrats, and beggars. No one was outside His reach; each person received individual attention.

Notice that in each case He used a different approach. We search in vain for a canned speech or "presentation" that Jesus always used. We can see an overall pattern, which we will look at in a moment, but His evangelistic method was customized to each person's need and unique situation. Jesus was driven by loving people, and each encounter was an opportunity for Him to show them God's love. As we explore this fourth core characteristic of Christlikeness, we can feel Jesus' passion and sense His urgency to reach people with the Good News of God's love.

In His inaugural message in His hometown, Jesus used Isaiah 61 as His launching pad and description of His ministry. Reading from verses 1-2 in front of the synagogue, Jesus said, "The Spirit of the Lord is on me, because he has anointed me to preach good news to the poor. He has sent me to proclaim freedom for the prisoners and recovery of sight for the blind, to release the oppressed" (Luke 4:18). Jesus was communicating "this is why I have come: I have been sent by the Holy Spirit to 'share God's good news with people.'"

Though no one there fully grasped all that Jesus was saying, we can look back now and see how this passage from Isaiah 61 would describe His ministry for the next three years. Jesus' ministry was a Spirit-led, Spirit-anointed, Spirit-sent ministry. Jesus spent His entire ministry, led by the Spirit, going from town to town sharing the Good News of God's love with person after person.

As Jesus followed the Spirit, the desire to reach more people with God's Good News meant never settling down in one location for too long. People in many of the towns begged for Jesus to stay, but He was resolute, driven by a clear purpose. Luke records one such example in Luke 4:42-43: "The people were looking for him and when they came to where he was, they tried to keep him from leaving them. But he said, 'I must preach the good news of the kingdom of God to the other towns also, *because that is why I was sent*'" (italics mine).

Jesus' sense of "being sent" by the Spirit, the knowledge that He was on a mission that must be fulfilled fueled His intentionality and gave Him laser-like focus. The message He was "sent" to deliver was the "good news" of the kingdom of God: that God loves you and invites you into His kingdom, so turn from your sin and surrender your life to the King. Every time you see the phrase "good news" or the word "gospel" in the New Testament, it translates the Greek word *euangelion*, the word from which we get our word "evangelism." To evangelize people is to "good news" them.

So when we say Jesus intentionally sought out people to show and share the Good News, we are saying Jesus intentionally evangelized. He saw Himself as being *sent* to evangelize, referring both to the Father and the Spirit as the "senders." Over sixty times, the word "send" is used in the New Testament to describe Jesus being sent or Jesus Himself sending His disciples to fulfill God's mission. For Him to use so much "sent" language reveals that intentional evangelism was a core characteristic of His life.

We too have been sent. Jesus said to His disciples in John 20:21, "As the Father has sent me, I am sending you." We must not wait for people to come to us; we must go to them and love them, build relationships with them, reach out to them, share and show the Good News with them.

Just as Jesus intentionally reached out to people, so you can see wise intentionality in how He went about developing them into disciples. Jesus began His ministry preaching and teaching to large groups of people, but mass evangelism wasn't His plan to reach the world. He quietly handpicked twelve men to be a part of His master plan to reach the world with the gospel. He poured His life into these men, building relationships with them, evangelizing them, apprenticing them, discipling them, and preparing them for ministry.

In Jesus' day, the word disciple had a very clear meaning: a disciple is one who *follows* his master (Mark 1:17) and *learns* from that master (Matthew 11:29) in order to *become* like that master (Luke 6:40). Jesus' goal was for His disciples to become like Him and disciple the next generation. Just before He left this world, He called these men together and gave them the Great Commission to go make disciples of all nations. Basically Jesus was saying, "Do what I've done; make disciples who will make disciples."

We can see five clear steps in Jesus' intentional method to share God's Good News and make disciples. These five steps serve as a great model for anyone today seeking to do the same. In the church I serve, I've organized our whole mission around these clear steps in evangelizing and discipling our generation. Just as Jesus was sent to share and show the Good News and make disciples, so He sends His disciples out to do the same.

1. Build

God's love is best understood through relationships, so Jesus' first step was to **build relationships**. The Incarnation, Jesus leaving heaven and becoming man, is the theological principle for building relationships with lost people in order to share the Good News. God didn't shout the gospel from heaven or drop a book out of the sky, He sent a person. Referring to Jesus, John 1:14 says, "The Word became flesh and made his dwelling among us." Jesus "moved into the neighborhood" and began to build relationships. When you read the four Gospels, you see that Jesus' favorite relationship-building tools were *serving people* and *asking questions*.

Serving People

Jesus said in Mark 10:45, "The Son of Man did not come to be served, but to serve." As we will see in more detail in the next chapter, Jesus was a Spirit-led servant. His serving ran the gamut from feeding hungry people to helping hurting people to healing the sick. Why did Jesus do this? Why did He not just "preach the gospel"? He did this because the Good News is something you share *and* show. This is a great model for us.

As we saw in Luke 4, Jesus said He came to "preach the good news," but if you continue to read you'll see that's not all He came to do. Most people who quote Luke 4:18, which says Jesus came to "preach the good news," leave off the rest of the passage that says He came to "release the oppressed." And in Isaiah 61, which Jesus was quoting, it is even clearer. In between "preach the good news" and "proclaim freedom for the captives" you have these words: "He has sent me to bind up the brokenhearted." Helping people was a vital part of Jesus' ministry; it was by no means "just preaching the good news." Page after page of the Gospels shows Jesus loving people, interacting with them, helping and healing, and along the way telling stories and teaching lessons about the kingdom of God. He proclaimed God's love *and* He demonstrated God's love as He served people.

Serving people is a simple and Christlike way to love people and build relationships. The old saying applies: "People don't care how much you know until they know how much you care." The apostle Paul said it like this: We can speak all kinds of truth and display all kinds of biblical knowledge that is accurate and exhaustive, but if we don't love people in tangible ways, we are "a resounding gong or clanging cymbal" (1 Corinthians 13:1).

In Acts 10:38, Peter provides an interesting summary of Jesus' ministry by reminding the people "how God anointed Jesus of Nazareth with the Holy Spirit and power, and how he went around <u>doing good</u>." Jesus' ministry of serving people and "doing good" impacted the people around Him. We can too. "Doing good" covers a lot of ground. It can range from helping your neighbors out when sickness and crisis comes to feeding people, or even something as small as helping your neighbors rake their leaves, shovel the snow off their driveway, or volunteer to watch their kids. Invite them over to your house and serve them a meal. Ask God to open your eyes to serving opportunities all around you at home, work, school, and the gym. Then pray that your serving will open up opportunities for relationship.

We hold an annual Serve Our City event where we ask the city what needs they have and go about meeting them in loving, effective ways. We plant flowers, paint houses, plant gardens, clean alleys, and pick up trash. Later in the year we hold an annual Family Fair for low-income families where we give away backpacks full of school supplies, free haircuts, free oil changes, free food, and invite local businesses to join in the fun of serving our community. We want to build relationships with individuals as well as with our city, and one of the best ways to do this is to serve people out of love.

Asking Questions

In addition to serving people, Jesus used questions to build relationships. As He reached out to people of all types, Jesus asked multiple levels of questions ranging from "Can I have a drink of water?" and "How do you read it?" to "What do you think?" and "Where's your faith?" In fact, these four questions are representative of all kinds of questions Jesus asked. If you were to take all the questions Jesus asked people and catalog them, you could summarize them all into four groups of questions:

1. Questions That Establish Contact ("Can I have a drink of water?"—John 4:7)
2. Questions That Expand Conversations ("How do you read it?"—Luke 10:26)
3. Questions That Explore Convictions ("What do you think?"—Matthew 22:42)
4. Questions That Extend Challenges ("Who do you say I am?"—Mark 16:15)

You and I can use this progression as we build redemptive relationships with people. Here are some examples of questions we can ask in each category:

1. **Questions That Establish Contact**
   a. Weather questions: nice day, huh? How long is this expected to last?
   b. What's your name? (prefaced by "Hi, I'm _____:")
   c. Where do you live/how long have you lived here?
   d. Did you see the game last night? Did you hear about . . . ? (Sports and current events questions.)

2. **Questions That Expand Conversations**
   a. What do you do for a living?
   b. Where did you grow up?

    c. Where did you get/how do you like that (tool, decoration, equipment, etc.)?

    d. Do you have any/how old are your kids?

    e. Will you help me with . . . ?

3. Questions That Explore Convictions

    a. Do you go to church anywhere?

    b. What do you believe/think about . . . (political issue, public debate, etc.)?

    c. Do you believe in God?

    d. What do you believe about Jesus?

    e. Have you ever read the Bible?

    f. How are you handling (a difficulty or trial they are going through)?

    g. How do you establish what is truth?

    h. Why do you believe that?

4. Questions That Extend Challenges

    a. Will you go to church/LifeGroup/event with me?

    b. Will you read this book?

    c. Have you ever considered Christ?

    d. Would you like to know more about Christ?

    e. Would you like to trust Christ as your Savior?

Jesus used questions to start relationships, build relationships, and deepen relationships. We can too. The Holy Spirit will lead us to ask the right questions. I know someone who, when he gets around non-believers, regularly prays and asks the Holy Spirit, "Help me to ask the right question." He believes the Holy Spirit is working and simply wants to cooperate with Him. After all, the Holy Spirit is the great evangelist. If we will listen, He will prompt us with the words to say, whether that is to ask a question, share the gospel, share our testimony, or invite someone to church.

Jesus built relationships because He loved people. So out of love for our family, friends, coworkers, and neighbors, we build relationships with them, serve them, model Christ to them, and explore what they believe about Jesus. This building of relationship can lead to spiritual conversations that directly relate to their spiritual questions and concerns and offer opportunities for us to lovingly share the gospel.

In asking these four kinds of questions, we might find that it takes us weeks or months before we can move to the fourth level of "extending a challenge." On the other hand, there are some situations where it is clear the Holy Spirit is leading us through these four levels in one setting and we can move to sharing the gospel and extending the challenge very quickly. The beauty of being led by the Spirit and using these questions is we are equipped to adjust as needed. For that resistant person, we go slower. For that person who has been prepared by the Holy Spirit to give their life to Christ right then and there, we are ready to share with them how to believe and trust Christ and extend the challenge to do so.

We always rejoice when a person responds to our challenge to believe in Christ, but what do we do with a person who isn't ready to surrender his life just yet? This is where most of the people with whom we share our faith are; they are in the *process* of considering Christ because coming to Christ is a process that culminates in their surrender to Christ. We believe the Spirit is drawing them and we want to cooperate with what He is doing. So we keep praying, sharing, witnessing, loving, serving, listening, and in the meantime "bring."

Back to Jesus and the Gospel records, this is where the disciples were: they had heard the gospel and were definitely interested, and they had started the process of believing, but Jesus knew they still didn't have saving, trusting belief as we will see below.

2. Bring

The next step for Jesus was **bring**. In John 2 we see Him bringing the disciples with Him to a wedding in Cana; in Matthew 9 He brings them to dinner at Matthew's house. In Mark 3 and 4 Jesus brings the disciples along with Him in the boat. In Luke 8 we see Jesus bring Peter and John with Him as He begins to heal a man's daughter.

What is Jesus doing? This kind of "bringing" is extending an invitation to take a next step in the relationship, to bring them to a place where they can more fully experience the presence of God. Remember, the disciples are learning to believe because believing is a process that culminates in an act of surrender to Christ as Lord. The Spirit of God opens people's eyes to the truth of the gospel and they put their faith in Christ. Though the disciples were growing in their belief, it wasn't until the night before He died that Jesus finally said to His disciples "You believe at last!" (John 16:31). Think of this, three years of seeing, hearing, and following the Son of God in the flesh, and yet they still didn't fully believe!

Jesus continued to bring the disciples along as He preached and served and healed people, showing and sharing the Good News. This is significant because Jesus knew they needed to "see" the gospel in action as well as "hear" it proclaimed. They needed to experience the presence of God as He touched people. In John 1 Jesus invites the disciples to "come and see." A few verses later, and also in Matthew 4, Mark 1, and Luke 5, He invites Peter and John to "follow me."

It is a very common misperception that Jesus merely "proclaimed" the gospel one time to the first disciples and they left their nets and followed Him. But by looking carefully at the Scripture passages we just referenced in the previous paragraph, you can see this is not the case. If you compare John's record in John 1 with the other Gospels (Matthew 4, Mark 1, and Luke 5) you can see that not only was this not the first time Peter and John had heard about/from Jesus, there is a very significant "bringing" episode as well. Let me show you.

In John 1, John is describing the first time Peter and Jesus met. John says that Andrew had been introduced to Jesus from John the Baptist, and then verse 41 says the first thing Andrew did was go find his brother Peter and tell him "we have found the Messiah!" Then you have these beautiful words in verse 42: "and he brought him to Jesus."

Andrew's words are the first example of someone other than Jesus practicing "bring." In fact, this is our clearest example of how you and I are to practice "bring."

Andrew gave a verbal witness to Peter and then practiced "bring" by bringing him to a place where he could meet Jesus. This is what we want to do: share our faith by giving a verbal witness and then bring our friends to a place where they can meet Jesus and hear more about Him. We don't know how long it was after that first meeting that Jesus said "follow me," but we do know that Mark 1:15 is not the first time Peter heard about or heard the teaching of Jesus. Peter heard teaching about the Good News and his brother brought him to Jesus. By the way, every time we see Andrew in John's Gospel, he is doing the same thing: bringing people to Jesus (see John 6:8 and 12:22). Andrew has left a legacy of practicing "bring."

In our church, we tell our people that when you have built a relationship, it is easier to "bring" your friend to a church service, LifeGroup, or some event at the church where they can more readily experience God's love and encounter Jesus. Over and over again the Gospels record people bringing people to Jesus. We want to both "bring" the Good News to people and "bring" people to Jesus. Helping people encounter the love of God is the foundation of our outreach; it is relational in orientation and motivated by love. We tell people to continue to "Build and Bring" until that person gives their life to Christ or begins to attend regularly and starts to experience the next stage: "Belong." This could take weeks or it could take years; what is important is that we are intentionally reaching out in love to **Build** redemptive relationships with lost people and **Bring** them into an environment where they can experience the power of **"Belonging,"** the supernatural and revolutionary love of a Christlike church.

3. Belong

Before I launch into describing how Jesus practiced what I call "**belong**," it is imperative that we stop and review how this word has come to be used by many of us today so we don't misunderstand what I am saying. Today, many people in the church use the word "belong" as a specialized, technical word to describe *being a member of a church*. That is fine and totally appropriate, but I want to use the word in its original meaning. To help someone feel like they belong is to accept them, to welcome them, to include them. This is what Jesus did. He accepted people, welcomed people, and invited people to "belong" before they believed. Jesus was teaching "belonging" long before there was formal church membership, and it is fascinating WHO He lets into His circle, who He invites to belong with Him.

Jesus lived in the day and age of the Pharisees, the most popular religious group in Israel. The Pharisees taught the people the Bible and set the rules (what Jesus called "traditions") for how the people of God were to act. The Pharisees were very clear that in order to be accepted by God, and therefore before you could be a part of their group, you had to "behave before you can belong." This philosophy of "behave before you can belong" is why "sinners, tax collectors, publicans, prostitutes, etc." were excluded and shunned. And this explains why the Pharisees were so upset with Jesus when He loved the "sinners" and accepted them *just as they were* and allowed them to hang out with Him, to "belong" with His group.

For Jesus, welcoming and accepting people just as they were *before they got their act together* was His way of introducing them to the power and truth of the gospel of God's love. After all, if we had to get it all together before we could belong, none of us would belong. This is why Paul says in Romans 15:7, "Accept one another, then, *just as Christ accepted you.*" How did Christ accept us? Did He wait for us to believe, wait for us to get cleaned up, wait for us to come to Him? Paul answers that question for us ten chapters earlier in Romans 5:8: "But God demonstrates his own love for us in this: While we were still sinners, Christ died for us."

It was while we were still sinners, before we believed, before we behaved, while we were still dead in our sins that Christ loved us, accepted us, and died for us.

The Pharisees just couldn't get past Jesus accepting people just as they were and letting them belong to his group. They were afraid of being contaminated by the "sinners." This short passage from Luke 5:30-32 describes the two views of "belonging" perfectly: "But the Pharisees and the teachers of the law who belonged to their sect complained to his disciples, 'Why do you eat and drink with tax collectors and "sinners"?' Jesus answered them, 'It is not the healthy who need a doctor, but the sick. I have not come to call the righteous, but sinners to repentance.'"

We may not see the significance of this passage in the twenty-first century, but those hearing it in the first century certainly did. In Jesus' day, *to eat with someone meant you saw them as almost family, as close friends; it was a way of saying "you belong."* And since the Pharisees knew this, THAT is why they were so upset with Jesus. Jesus let people belong before they behaved. Jesus accepted people just as they were. Not only did He accept them, Jesus *loved* people just the way they were. Notice how this passage ends in verse 32: repentance. Jesus loves and accepts people just as they are ... but too much to leave them that way. He accepts us as we are but calls us to repentance, to turn from our sin and surrender our life to Him.

The church is supposed to be the body of Christ on earth. Just like Jesus, we are to love and accept people just as they are, but we love them too much to leave them that way. We say, "Come as you are, you'll be loved." We don't say, "Clean up and then you can come be with us." We tell our people "bring your friends just as they are." They will hear a preacher lovingly preach the gospel of "while we were yet sinners Christ died for us." They will hear a preacher confirm the same thing their friend said to them when they witnessed and shared the gospel one on one: "God loves you and sent His Son to die for you; quit running and surrender your life to Him."

Jesus knew the power of doing life together, that the most important things in life are often "caught" as well as "taught." He wanted His disciples to feel the love of God, to see kingdom values lived out, to catch the vision of what He was all about. The best way to do that was to go beyond the formal teaching times and invite the disciples to experience the power of **belonging**.

In Mark 3:14 Jesus calls the disciples into this next level of relationship. Notice the language used: "He went up on a mountainside and called to him those he wanted, and they came to him. He appointed twelve—designating them apostles—*that they might be with him*" (italics mine). When Jesus invited the disciples to "be with him," He was inviting them to hang out with Him, to do life together. The goal was for them to "believe," and even back then, as is true today, many people want to belong before they believe. As they shared life together, they watched and listened to Jesus and began to experience the love and grace of God like never before.

Before He ever taught about the Holy Spirit, Jesus wanted the disciples to experience the work of the Spirit in knitting a group of people together. This climaxed in the book of Acts, but He was already at work with the disciples now, giving them this sense of belonging as they hung out with Jesus every day, day after day. A lot can happen when people spend significant amounts of time together: observations are made, impressions are formed, questions get asked, and life-on-life learning takes place.

Recently I visited one of our campuses in the Dominican Republic and some church plants we are sponsoring in Vietnam. In each case these small (but growing!) groups of people had already begun to manifest the supernatural and revolutionary love of a Christlike, Spirit-led church. They were practicing "Build and Bring" and the unsaved were coming, quickly sensing the power of "Belong" as they gathered to eat together and fellowship together. Just last night I was at our Santo Domingo (Dominican Republic) campus with

Pastor Pedro "Tito" Rosario. As their young and developing worship band played in the streets of their neighborhood, the crowd was mixed with "believers" and "belongers." The "belongers" were those attracted by the music but captured by the love of the believers, and who attended their church and neighborhood parties.

Even though (or perhaps because) I couldn't understand their language, I could see "belonging" happening right before my eyes as this Acts-type church loved on their friends and neighbors. It's no surprise that a steady stream of people are coming to Christ and leaving the cults and superstitious beliefs prevalent in that area. The excitement surrounding this campus is undeniable and extremely contagious.

The same thing is happening in the church plants we are sponsoring in Vietnam. The leader, Pastor Minh Dang, is bringing a revolution of love to that country as he plants what he calls "love churches" all over Vietnam. As I traveled throughout the country with Pastor Minh, I saw the fruits of their method which I would describe as simply "loving people, praying for people and sharing Christ with people." Powerful. Shouldn't we all be "love churches"?

The "belong" stage is a powerful time in the life of a person who is exploring faith in Christ. Churches today need to intentionally provide "belong" opportunities where newcomers can "taste and see that the Lord is good" (Psalm 34:8)," where they can feel the love and experience the power of the presence of the Spirit of God in a community of believers. This is why our churches need to be sensitive to seekers, explaining the gospel and teaching from God's Word so that the Spirit of God can use the Word of God and the love of the people of God to draw lost people to Christ.

Some claim the church should only be for believers, basing their claim on the grounds that they don't see any examples of unbelievers in New Testament churches. This is odd since the only passage in the New Testament that describes in detail what actually happened in a first-century church service *includes* unbelievers! First Corinthians 14 describes how Paul was telling the people that in their *church services* they should be sensitive to unbelievers and those who don't understand:

> Tongues, then, are a sign, not for believers but for unbelievers; prophecy, however, is for believers, not for unbelievers. So if the whole church comes together and everyone speaks in tongues, and some who do not understand or some unbelievers come in, will they not say that you are out of your mind? But if an unbeliever or someone who does not understand comes in while everybody is prophesying, he will be convinced by all that he is a sinner and will be judged by all, and the secrets of his heart will be laid bare. So he will fall down and worship God, exclaiming, "God is really among you!"
>
> 1 Corinthians 14:22-25

In a nutshell, this is one of the things we want to see happen in our church services: an unbeliever comes in, is convinced by the Holy Spirit that he is a sinner, and falls down in surrender, exclaiming "God is really among you!"

God wants us to bring unbelievers to church. And He wants believers to love them, accept them, welcome them, and help them feel a sense of belonging so they sense the love of God and surrender their life to Him. But some say unbelievers can't worship God. I agree. But they can witness us worshiping and they can sense the power and presence of God. In fact, the best place for an unbeliever to sense that God is real is in a powerful worship service! This is why worship can lead to evangelism (see Isaiah 6:1-8, Psalm 40:3, Psalm 67, Matthew 28:17 and 19ff) and why we must welcome unbelievers in our midst and help them feel the "belonging" love of God.

Perhaps one of the best pictures of the power of "belonging" is what happens in the Christian home. Godly parents lovingly show and share the Good News of Christ with their kids until the day comes when that child surrenders his or her life to Jesus Christ. Imagine a parent saying "you can't belong to this family until you behave or believe like we do." No, it's the incubating, nurturing, belonging love of the parent that leads them to believe! The church is to be an "incubator for the lost," nurturing unbelievers with the love of God, nourishing them with grace and truth so they will believe the Good News!

In the church, the Belong stage has a wide spectrum of people ranging from those just beginning to attend regularly but who still have lots of questions, all the way to those who have attended regularly for years but are still not yet involved beyond Sunday morning attendance. Within this stage of "Belong" we want to help people move from Fringe to Friends to Family. Because some people can get stuck in this stage, there needs to be a clear step to the next stage. It is paramount that we love and pray and share with someone in the Belong stage until they put their faith in Christ and **Believe**. We want to keep moving people to the next stage of development.

4. Believe

According to the Gospel of Mark, Jesus began His public ministry calling people to "believe" (Mark 1:15). A study of the word "believe" in the Gospels reveals it was the topic of discussion for Jesus in relationship after relationship. He challenged people to believe, called them to believe, and preached and taught the need to believe. But even with this emphasis, it took a long time for the disciples to get to the place where they believed. As seen earlier, it was the night before He went to the cross that Jesus exclaimed to the disciples: "You believe at last!" (John 16:31). Jesus knew that believing is a process. He was patient with the disciples and we must be patient too.

In Luke 8 Jesus tells the story of the seed (the Word of God) landing on different soils (our hearts), explaining the process of believing while at the same time warning of Satan's attempts to block belief. In verse 12 He says, "Those along the path are the ones who hear, and then the devil comes and takes away the word from their hearts, so that they may not believe and be saved." We need to keep sharing the gospel, keep bringing people to hear the Word preached, keep sowing the seed of the Word, keep watering the seed with praying and loving, all with the goal that they will believe!

The apostle John said that his whole purpose in writing the fourth Gospel was that we "may believe that Jesus is the Christ, the Son of God, and that by believing you may have life in his name" (John 20:31). Jesus said He came "that we might believe," and in John 17:20 He prayed for all future believers: "I pray also for those who will believe in me through their message." Jesus was praying for us and the people we are trying to lead to Christ!

Everything changes once someone believes the gospel. The message of Jesus isn't an ethic to aspire to or an appeal to do good deeds; it is a way of living that is based on believing what Jesus said about God, ourselves, and the world. As we love people through **Build**, **Bring** and **Belong**, we are helping them develop certain beliefs about God. The Holy Spirit is working in their lives convicting them of sin and forming faith in them, enabling and drawing them to take the step of faith.

This step of faith is **Believe**. This is where the person gets serious about their faith, where they wrestle seriously with what they believe and make a commitment to surrender their lives to Christ. To believe is to cross the line of faith, to surrender completely to Christ and put our trust in Him.

This crisis of belief is the core issue in each person's relationship with God, and we need to continue to build, bring, and help them belong as they work through what they believe. Of course, you may meet a person who is ready to put their faith in Christ the first time you meet them. Others may be slower to respond, and still others may seem like they will never believe. But we keep bringing, we keep loving, we keep sharing our faith, and we keep praying that they will believe. When a person cooperates with the Spirit and takes this step of faith, believing, it launches them into the **Become** phase.

5. Become

The commitment to put our faith in Christ, to believe, marks the beginning of the journey of **becoming** like Christ, a walk of faith in which every step involves believing and becoming. Far too many churches act as if "believe is the end goal" when in fact the Bible makes clear that the goal is for us to become like Christ. Romans 8:29 (NLT) says, "For God knew his people in advance, and he chose them to become like his Son." The premise of this book is that God has designed us to become like Christ, and the only way that happens is as we learn to cooperate with the Holy Spirit. Jesus didn't see believing as the goal but as a means to the goal. As we learn to cooperate with the Holy Spirit, He forms Christlikeness in us; the Spirit is the one who makes us more like Christ. Luke 6:40 (NLT) says, "The student [disciple] who is fully trained will become like the teacher." Ephesians 4:15 (NLT) says maturity is about "becoming more and more in every way like Christ."

(I won't elaborate any more right here about **become** since this whole book is devoted to the process of **becoming** more like Christ, describing how the Holy Spirit is working in us, and what becoming like Christ looks like. But if you are interested in discovering your next step in becoming like Christ, you may want to try a tool I designed called the Next Step Survey at http://opendoor.tv/nextstep/.)

In the final chapter, I describe how this works in our church and explain how the whole process is driven by love. We created a graphic with the 5B's centered around a heart to remind us that love reaches out to Build, Bring, then helps people Belong, Believe and Become:

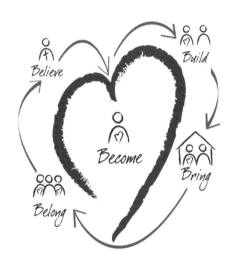

Go Make Disciples

Just before He ascended into heaven, Jesus commanded His disciples to "go make disciples." These five steps, Build, Bring, Belong, Believe, and Become, provide a process by which we can obey Him. We can always be working with a person or several people through these stages. We know that the Holy Spirit is the great evangelist and He invites us into His work. These five steps give us specific ways to cooperate with what He is doing. He does His work of conviction, leading to repentance and saving, and we do our work of loving, sharing, witnessing, serving, and praying. The 5B's don't have to be in a rigid order; God will do His unique work in the life of people. But if we are aware of the stages, we can cooperate with the Holy Spirit as He also chooses to use us to love, share, witness, serve, and eventually lead someone to Christ.

Once we notice this 5B pattern, it is remarkable how often people's path to faith is marked by these stages. It was in my family's path to faith in the opening story of this chapter, and it is for countless others. We have been using this process in our church since I first came up with it in 2004 and we have seen it work in person after person as they come to Christ!

Spirit-led Evangelism

Not only is the Holy Spirit at work in the lives of pre-Christians drawing them to Christ, but since intentional evangelism is one of the core Christlike characteristics, He is at work in us, leading us, guiding us, and making us more like Christ as we reach out to them.

When we are becoming more like Christ, there should be an intentionality about our lives to see people come to Christ. The Holy Spirit will lead us as He fills us. As we learn to practice Spiritual Breathing, He will lead us and prompt us into opportunities to share the love of God with people who have not yet heard the Good News.

Jesus said that when the Holy Spirit comes, He will give us power to witness, power to cooperate with what

He is doing. The Bible makes it clear that Jesus practiced intentional evangelism as He was led by the Holy Spirit. He modeled doing evangelism in the power of the Spirit and taught His disciples then and now (us) to do the same.

The Book of Acts is the story of the disciples and the first Christians listening to the promptings of the Holy Spirit and evangelizing their world with the Good News of Jesus Christ. One of my favorite episodes is in Acts 8 where the Holy Spirit leads Philip to share the Good News of Christ with a man traveling through the area. We are first introduced to Philip in Acts 6 where he is described as a man "full of the Spirit" (Acts 6:3). When we live full of the Spirit, God will lead us into a life of adventure.

One day God directed Philip very specifically to head down to a certain road. God never told him what was going to happen; he just gave him directions to head down south. Philip obeyed. I love how verse 27 then says "on his way" he met a man from Ethiopia traveling down the road. God led Philip's path to directly intersect with this man's path, and "on his way" a divine appointment unfolded. Watch how the Holy Spirit leads Philip to a ready-made opportunity to share the Good News of Christ: "The Spirit told Philip, 'Go to that chariot and stay near it.' Then Philip ran up to the chariot and heard the man reading Isaiah the prophet. 'Do you understand what you are reading?' Philip asked. 'How can I,' he said, 'unless someone explains it to me?' So he invited Philip to come up and sit with him."

The man "just happened" to be reading Isaiah 53, and Philip, led by the Spirit, explained how this passage was a prophecy about Jesus and led him to Christ right in the chariot! The process is simple: the Holy Spirit led and Philip obeyed.

Acts is an exciting adventure through twenty-eight chapters of Spirit-breathed evangelism. But the Holy Spirit didn't stop with Acts 28. Today we are living in "Acts 29" and God is still leading and prompting His people to share the Good News of Christ with a world desperate to know Him. Spiritual Breathing helps us to pay attention to the promptings of the Holy Spirit, and as we learn to listen to Him, He will lead us in exciting ways.

I consider it an honor to be a friend of John Beckett, a bestselling author of several books including *Loving Monday* and *Mastering Monday*. John is one of the most unassuming men you will ever meet. Though he's a graduate of MIT and a very successful businessman, John is a humble man who has learned to live in the power of the Holy Spirit. He travels all around the world helping people integrate their faith with the rest of their life, especially in their jobs. I highly recommend reading John's books, but the story I am going to tell isn't in them. It is one of the most exciting stories of evangelism in the last hundred years if not more. And it all starts with him obeying a simple prompting of the Holy Spirit.

John was deeply affected by the February 1, 2003, tragedy of the Columbia Space Shuttle and the death of seven astronauts who were as he said "facing eternity in a moment." He felt the Spirit prompting him to write a little booklet called "Coming Home" telling his story of coming to Christ and communicating the gospel in clear, nonreligious but biblically sound language. The booklet saw significant distribution but then a businessman from California who was very savvy with the Internet encouraged John to format his message for a website. They eventually created a site called lifesgreatestquestion.com and, as he says, "then the fun began."

At the time of this writing, on any given day, of the billion or so people searching the Internet, he said over a million are searching for answers to deeper issues like "the meaning of life." Over 750,000 people per month are visiting John's site, from 191 different countries. In the last month more than 65,000 people around the world indicated a decision to follow Christ through his website. That's 2,166 people a day, the size of megachurch in the United States!

Next he decided to try developing a message that could be used as an advertisement on mobile devices since in most countries phones are subsidized through advertisements. He saw 18,000 people indicate a decision for Christ in one month!

John says it all started with a prompting of the Holy Spirit. But here's the key: we have to pay attention to these promptings and obey what the Spirit says. Who knows what God will do when we simply follow up on simple promptings of the Spirit? Maybe it's not to start a website, create a video, or write a pamphlet. Maybe it's simply to talk to your neighbor, bring over some cookies, or invite them for a BBQ. Whatever the Spirit is prompting you to do, do it! Who could have known that when John Beckett came to Christ years ago, God would someday use him to help millions of people come to Christ?

Who knows what God wants to do through you as you learn to cooperate with the promptings of the Holy Spirit? Friend, if you are a Christian, the Spirit of the Lord is upon you and He has anointed you to bring people the Good News! Join the adventure!

Breathing Example

I met a couple after one of our services and quickly discovered that the man not only wasn't a Christian, he wasn't interested in becoming a Christian. His wife had dragged him down to talk to the preacher and he was just pacifying her by even coming down. We dialogued back and forth and every time he spoke, I breathed a quick prayer asking God to open his heart. Slowly, I sensed him warming up. I asked him if he had ever thought of giving his life to Christ and he said he had, but didn't think he ever would. I asked him if he knew what it meant to surrender his life to Christ and when he hesitated, I asked him if I could share with him how he could put his faith in Christ. He seemed reluctant but willing. I shared about God's love, our sin and our need for Christ. When I was done, I asked him if he would like to turn from his self-centeredness and follow Jesus. He said very plainly, "no."

Just at that moment, I sensed the Holy Spirit say, "ask him if you can pray for him to <u>want to</u> surrender." I had never asked that of anyone in the past, and it seemed to me to be a crazy request, but I was pretty sure it was the Holy Spirit. So I decided to go for it and said, "could I pray with you and ask God to give you the desire to <u>want to</u> surrender to him?" He looked at me funny and said, "I guess." So I did. And God did. When I was done praying, I asked him if he was ready to surrender and he said as firmly and confidently as I've ever heard: "Yes I am." I led him in a prayer of repentance and surrender and he began to cry, broken over his sin and rebellion. It was powerful. Beautiful. Miraculous. God saved him and changed his heart. (He now serves on our tech team and is a table leader at Alpha, an outreach ministry we hold at our church.)

Breathing Exercise

God wants to lead us by His Holy Spirit to show and share the Good News of His love. He will lead us to love people, build relationships with people, serve people, ask them questions, and listen. He will prompt us to take evangelistic steps with people and reach them with the Good News. As you practice Spiritual Breathing, pay attention to the breathing in and breathing out cycle, using the natural rhythm of your breathing to focus your prayers.

Here is some language to guide your Spiritual Breathing in intentional evangelism:

- As we breathe in, we want to receive the Holy Spirit and say: *"Holy Spirit, breathe in me Your power to witness."*
- As we breathe out, we want to remove any sin or toxins and say: *"I confess my fear and doubt."*
- As we breathe in again, we want to receive the Holy Spirit and say: *"Holy Spirit, I receive Your power to witness."*

- As we breathe out again, we want to thank God and say: *"Holy Spirit, thank You for Your presence and power."*

Alternate words as we breathe in:

> *"Holy Spirit, breathe in me love for this person."*
> *"Holy Spirit, breathe in me a good question to ask."*
> *"Holy Spirit, breathe in me Your words."*
> *"Holy Spirit, breathe in me love, power, and a sound mind."*

Alternate words as we breathe out:

> *"I confess my excuses."*
> *"I confess my lack of love."*
> *"I confess my self-centeredness."*
> *"I confess my insecurities."*

Feel free to add, elaborate, or edit as needed. Remember, the Holy Spirit wants to shape our hearts and minds through sharing our faith as He makes us more like Christ. We just need to learn to *breathe.*

SECTION FOUR

· ·

Living Surrendered

CHAPTER ELEVEN

Spirit-led Servant

Core Christlike Characteristic: Jesus was a Spirit-led, Spirit-empowered Servant

B ooks written on the lives of great leaders never mention, let alone emphasize, that the leader was *being* led when they made their most important contribution to society. The whole point of recognizing them as great leaders is that they *led* not followed. And yet when we come to the greatest, most influential leader ever, Jesus Christ, one of the core characteristics of His life is that He was led by another. When He made His greatest contribution to society, He was *being* led by someone else.

In this chapter we will explore the leadership of the Holy Spirit in the life of Jesus, which is the fifth core Christlike characteristic. We will discover that this characteristic was the secret to His remarkable life while on earth. It wove through all of the other characteristics and in fact is essential to each of them.

What was true in the life of Jesus can be true in our lives as well. The adventure of becoming like Christ from start to finish is a Spirit-led journey. We can't become like Christ without the Holy Spirit, so learning how to be a Holy Spirit-led servant will be central to every step we take on the adventure. We too must learn how to live surrendered to the power of the Holy Spirit in our lives.

Because we have been raised in a society that prizes individualism and ambition, the biggest struggle for most of us as Christians is in learning how to cooperate with the Holy Spirit, living surrendered to His leadership. But once we do, it unlocks the secret to Christlikeness.

When Jesus called His disciples to follow Him and learn from Him, it was so they could become like Him. But unlike disciples of other great rabbis and leaders, Jesus never intended for His disciples to merely memorize His words and mimic His actions. He wanted them to grasp the skill of living surrendered to the leadership of the Holy Spirit.

No amount of anxious striving on the part of the disciple makes him or her like Christ; sanctification is the work of the Holy Spirit. And yet this work is not done apart from us but in cooperation with us. The secret to living the Christlike life is learning how to cooperate with the Holy Spirit, how to breathe in His sanctifying power and move in the rhythms of His grace. Jesus wanted to pass on this skill, this way of living, to His disciples. He begins by modeling what He will teach.

Jesus demonstrated a Spirit-led life long before He began to teach about it. In fact, as Luke records the beginning of Jesus' ministry, the dominating theme is the leadership and work of the Holy Spirit in Jesus' life. Fresh out of the baptism waters where the Holy Spirit is a part of inaugurating Jesus' ministry, He begins His ministry in Luke 4 with a chapter full of references to the Holy Spirit. Each of these references to the Spirit has different descriptors associated with it that yields powerful truths.

Verse 1 starts off with the words "Jesus, *full of the Holy Spirit*, returned from the Jordan and was *led by the Spirit.*" After being tempted by the devil in the desert, verse 14 says, "Jesus returned to Galilee in the *power of the Spirit.*" Then four verses later, quoting Isaiah 61, Jesus announces, "*the Spirit of the Lord is upon me because he has anointed me.*"

It is very clear that here at the beginning of Jesus' ministry Luke means for his readers to see that whatever Jesus was doing was through the "power" of the Spirit. This power was due to the "filling," "leading," and "anointing" of the Holy Spirit in His life. These are fascinating, colorful words, and if we want to move in the power of the Spirit, it's worth looking at each of these three words more closely. As we learn to cooperate with the Holy Spirit in our lives, these three ideas will play a key role.

Filled with the Holy Spirit

The language of being filled with the Spirit is familiar language in the Bible, but in the Old Testament it is only used to describe the Spirit filling someone temporarily or to accomplish a timely, specific task, such as speaking a word of prophecy (Micah 3:8) or crafting something for God's temple (Exodus 31:3). John the Baptist and Jesus are the first ones to live their lives "full of the Spirit" on a continuing basis.

Most people tend to think of this word "full" as filling a container (like filling a cup, or in biblical times, filling a jar or goatskin with water), but the Greek language has a different word for that kind of filling. The word used here in Luke 4:1 for "full" means to be "thoroughly permeated with" or "completely occupied with." Think "full" like a sponge that is filled with water; it's the idea of being saturated with something.

There's a beautiful parallel in our bodies to this kind of "full." When we breathe, we fill our lungs with air and the oxygen saturates the millions of alveoli lining our lungs (which are like little microscopic sponges). As these alveoli are saturated with oxygen, we say our lungs are "full" of air.

When we breathe spiritually, we fill our lives with the Holy Spirit and the Spiritual Oxygen saturates our heart and mind and soul. He cleanses us from the inside out, removing the toxins and permeating our lives with His presence. Once more we see how the Holy Spirit is Spiritual Oxygen, filling our lives with His life-giving presence.

Every Christian is filled with the Spirit when they become a Christian. The filling of the Holy Spirit is what applies the transforming power of God's grace to our hearts and lives causing us to be born again. Without being filled with the Holy Spirit, we cannot become a Christian. But the Bible makes it very clear that being filled with the Holy Spirit is not a one-time event. Ephesians 5:18, written to people who are already Christians, is best translated as a command—"be being filled with the Holy Spirit"— and communicates "keep on being filled with the Spirit over and over again on an ongoing, repetitive basis." This repetitive process describes perfectly what happens when we practice Spiritual Breathing and enables us to live the way Christ intends for His disciples to live. In fact, the only way to live the Christian life is to breathe the Holy Spirit.

Led by the Holy Spirit

Not only was Jesus full of the Spirit, Luke tells us in the same sentence He was "led by the Spirit." Why the need for both phrases? There are similarities between the two, and one does lead into the other, but the differences are worth noting. "Full" has to do with content or substance; "led" has to do with direction. "Full" is descriptive language; "led" is active language. When I am full of the Spirit, it is easier to be led by the Spirit. Luke uses the word "led" in 4:1 in a specific Greek tense that indicates something that was happening "continuously." Jesus was continuously being led by the Spirit. As Jesus went from town to town, He was being led by the Spirit. As He moved from person to person to minister to them God's love, He was being led by the Spirit.

God's desire is that we live our lives being led by the Spirit. In fact, Romans 8:14 says, "All those who are led by the Holy Spirit are children of God." The Spirit is the dominating influence in our lives, whispering His holy promptings throughout the day. As the Holy Spirit leads in a person's life, He will prompt them to a particular action whether it's an act of worship, serving someone, sharing the gospel, or a simple act of love.

As I was writing this, my wife, Andrea, was involved in an example of this simple act of love prompted by the

Spirit. Earlier today she felt a leading of the Spirit to send a text message of encouragement to a friend in another state. She promptly obeyed and sent the text. Within an hour she received a grateful, emotional response. It read, "Our hearts are lifted! I just shared your response with my husband. ☺ You have no idea . . . or I guess you do! That's why God spoke to you!!! Tears keep filling my eyes. OXOXOXOX!!!"

This couple was going through a tremendous difficulty fourteen hundred miles away. It was weighing them down with discouragement. But God is not bound by the limitations of geography, so He prompted Andrea in Ohio to send a little word of encouragement to her friend Carmen in Colorado. Led by the Spirit, she was used by God in a significant moment in this couple's life. It didn't make the newspaper, CNN didn't send a reporter out to interview Andrea, and she probably won't go on a book tour talking about it. (But it did make my book!) These moments don't have to be headline moments, but they are important moments, and this one was especially important to our friends in Colorado.

The Spirit may prompt you to send an email, write a letter, make a phone call, visit a friend, bring a neighbor food, or witness to a coworker. He may prompt you to pray, give, listen, sing, serve, share, or worship.

Anointed by the Holy Spirit

As we saw earlier, when Jesus spoke in Luke 4 He was quoting directly from the first verses of Isaiah 61, and

He says "the Spirit of the Lord is on me" for a very clear purpose. In most English Bibles, that purpose is "to preach good news." In both the Hebrew and the Greek, the idea is that the Spirit has anointed Jesus to "bring" good news to the poor. "Bringing" includes preaching but is much more than preaching. Perhaps that is what St. Francis of Assisi was thinking when he penned his famous line: "Preach the gospel at all times; if necessary use words." Jesus said, "I have been sent to preach and bring and share and demonstrate the good news."

In my first sermon as the pastor of the church I currently serve, I began a teaching series from Isaiah 61. I stood in front of them and said, "I am anointed; the Spirit of the Lord is upon me." I knew it would cause some to be a little startled. People were thinking to themselves, *Who does this guy think he is? How audacious that he thinks he is anointed.* After a dramatic pause for effect, I said, "And *you* are anointed. If you are truly born again and have surrendered your life to Christ, then the Spirit of God is in you and upon you and has anointed you; we must learn to live surrendered to the Holy Spirit." Then I challenged them that we might be a church led by, filled with, and anointed by the Holy Spirit.

Christians are supposed to live in the anointing, in the power of the Holy Spirit, moving and flowing in the strength of the Holy Spirit. Jesus lived His life as a model of how we're to live our lives, but He didn't do it in His own strength. Neither will we cver be able to live the Christlike life in our own strength. To be like Jesus, we need to live in the anointing. I know that phrase sounds super-spiritual, and it has been used to endorse some crazy behavior, but the word "anointed" is very biblical.

Anointing is a concept that gets its beginning in the Old Testament. The New Testament then builds on this Old Testament foundation. The concept of anointing carried a clear meaning that contained four ideas. The basic word "anoint" meant to apply olive oil on people (such as priests or kings) or objects (such as sacred instruments used in the temple) to set them apart for God's service. The importance wasn't in the oil itself, but what it signified. In 1 Samuel 16:13, the prophet Samuel anoints David as the next king of Israel. Watch what happens: "So Samuel took the horn of oil and anointed him in the presence of his brothers, and from that day on the Spirit of the LORD came upon David in power." So, first, anointing meant:

to receive God's power.

Notice the direct correlation between "anointing," the "Spirit of the Lord," and the "power" he received. As we have seen throughout this book, the power of God comes with the presence of the Holy Spirit. Therefore, this power was not inherent power in the person but delegated power from the Holy Spirit. As king, David and the other kings were to represent God. This is true of anyone else who was anointed, such as priests. They represented God's presence. This is true for you and me; God anoints us that we might receive His power and use that power to represent His presence. So, secondly, anointing meant:

to represent God's presence.

People anointed by God were anointed to receive God's power and represent God's presence in order to *do* something; there is action here. Look at the very next chapter in 1 Samuel after David was anointed, chapter 17. Here's God's newly anointed man, he's received God's power to represent God's presence, and these two ideas contribute to the third aspect of anointing. What is chapter 17 all about? David and Goliath! First Samuel 17:45-47 records David's words in response to Goliath defying the Lord. In verse 47 he tells Goliath that "all those gathered here will know that it is not by sword or spear that the LORD saves; for the battle is the LORD's, and he will give all of you into our hands."

Notice the phrase "the battle is the LORD's." Where did he get this idea? The text doesn't say David checked in with God or that God sent him. It seems we are left with one of two realistic possibilities. Either this idea came from God or from David. But God never asks anybody to fight His battles. David himself says the battle is the Lord's. David is going into this moment with such confidence of the outcome because he is responding to something God has prompted him to do. This is not David-initiated action but God-initiated direction. David responds to God's initiation. So the third aspect of anointing was:

to respond to God's promptings.

Verse 47 teaches us something else as well. When David says "the battle is the LORD's," he is reflecting that the bigger picture here is fulfilling God's purposes. This is very significant: David is just God's servant to fulfill God's purposes. All of these three aspects of the anointing find their climax in the fourth:

to realize God's purposes.

Now let's go back to Luke 4 and put this together: *the anointing of the Spirit is to receive God's power to represent God's presence by responding to God's promptings so that we can realize God's purposes.* Jesus is saying, "the Spirit has anointed me to receive God's power to represent God's presence. I live led by the Spirit, responding to His promptings so I can realize God's purposes." The filling and anointing of the Spirit enables us to be led by the Spirit so we can move in the power of the Spirit. This is how the Spirit worked in Jesus' life, and it is how He wants to work in our lives.

I have been asked numerous times over the years, "How does this work out in practical ways in my day-to-day life? How can I learn to be led by the Spirit?" The answer is found in exploring more closely how we live our lives on a day-to-day basis, how we organize our day, and the kind of functional environment we gravitate toward. Some of us are very structured people while others of us are more spontaneous. God has wired us so that we all fit on a continuum somewhere between spontaneous and structured. It is easier for us to sense the leading of the Holy Spirit in ways that fit how God has wired us.

If we are more spontaneous, we will tend to sense the leading of the Spirit in spontaneous ways. If we are more structured, we may be very uncomfortable with and even suspicious of "spontaneous promptings" of the Spirit. Likewise, if we are more structured, we will sense the leading of the Spirit in ways that are much more structured and predictable. The Holy Spirit works and leads in both ways, but most people have one environment that they prefer over another. Neither preference is right or wrong, it's just how you are wired. However, for most of us, our greatest potential to grow in being led by the Spirit is to develop the area *opposite* our natural preference. Maturity in recognizing the voice of the Spirit is measured by our ability to hear and obey His leading in both structured and spontaneous ways.

Let's explore these two environments in which the Holy Spirit leads us. If we want to be led by the Spirit in our daily lives, we must structure our life around the leadership of the Spirit. We must deliberately, purposely work a plan that trains us to live led by the Holy Spirit. We will learn to hear His voice, obey His voice, and live surrendered to His voice in our life.

Learning the Language of the Spirit

The most important step in learning to be led by the Spirit is learning the language of the Holy Spirit. When we learn any language, we learn vocabulary, grammar, and syntax. The same is true in learning the language of the Spirit. As babies grow into toddlers and begin to learn their first language, they learn how to recognize and distinguish sounds and words, vocalize sounds, words and phrases, and categorize and assign meanings. We go through these same stages as we learn the language of the Spirit; it all begins with listening. Listening is the most important skill in learning the language of the Spirit. Learning to live attentive to the promptings of the Spirit is a skill that will reap tremendous fruit in our lives.

While listening is the most important *skill*, the most important *tool* to facilitate this training is the Word of God. The Spirit speaks through the Word. The Holy Spirit inspired the Word of God to be written, illuminates the Word of God so we can grasp what it says, and interprets the Word of God so we can understand what it means. We learn the language of the Spirit of God in the Word of God. The best way to learn the language of the Holy Spirit involves reading, studying, meditating on, memorizing, and praying the Word of God. If we want to hear from God, we must build the structure of Scripture into our lives.

For two thousand years, spiritual directors of all kinds have used the structure of meditating on and praying the Scriptures to teach people to learn the language of the Spirit. The Word of God is the native tongue of the Holy Spirit. As we learn the language of the Holy Spirit, the Spirit uses the truth of Scripture to do some very significant things in our lives. Through the Scripture He will:

- guide us. "When he, the Spirit of truth, comes, he will guide you into all truth" (John 16:13).

- teach us. "But the Counselor, the Holy Spirit . . . will teach you all things and will remind you of everything I have said to you" (John 14:26).
- correct and train us. "All Scripture is God-breathed and is useful for teaching, rebuking, correcting and training in righteousness" (2 Timothy 3:16).
- convict us. "When he comes, he will convict the world of guilt in regard to sin and righteousness and judgment" (John 16:8).
- reveal who God is to us. "God has revealed it to us by his Spirit. The Spirit searches all things, even the deep things of God" (1 Corinthians 2:10).
- strengthen us. "I pray that out of his glorious riches he may strengthen you with power through his Spirit in your inner being" (Ephesians 3:16).
- make us more like Christ. "And as the Spirit of the Lord works within us, we become more and more like him and reflect his glory even more" (2 Corinthians 3:18).

We are able to recognize the leadership of the Holy Spirit as we fill our minds with the language of the Spirit through an ongoing, steady diet of feeding on the Word of God. In the pages of the Bible we see the Holy Spirit speaking, guiding, and leading through many different ways: visions, dreams, prophetic words, angels, an audible voice, or a silent, internal voice.

Building a structure of daily Bible reading and meditation into our lives is a very significant part of learning the language of the Spirit. As we get better at recognizing the language of the Spirit through familiarity with the Word of God, we can learn to recognize His voice in other ways as well. These are the "spontaneous promptings" of the Spirit. Most of the promptings of the Spirit will fall under two general categories: praying and serving.

Galatians 4:6 (NLT) says, "Because we are his children, God has sent the Spirit of his Son into our hearts, prompting us to call out, 'Abba, Father.'" These promptings to pray include not only the urge to pray but may involve the Spirit prompting the very words of our prayers. Deeper yet, He may prompt Spirit-led intercession beyond words. Paul describes this in Romans 8:26: "We do not know what we ought to pray for, but the Spirit himself intercedes for us with groans that words cannot express." There are many other "messages" the Spirit will speak to us through these promptings to pray, such as warnings, comfort, guidance, rebuke, problem solving, conviction, direction, or encouragement. These messages may be for us or for someone else.

Spirit-led Servant

But the Spirit will not only prompt us to pray, He will also prompt us to serve. One of the marks that a person is being led by the Holy Spirit is whether or not that person is being led to serve others out of love. Too many people today want the leading of the Spirit or want to hear from God for self-centered purposes. The fruit of the Spirit is love, and love is an other-centered orientation, so when the Spirit leads He will lead us to love and serve others.

216

In fact, the clearest evidence that you are being led by the Spirit is the orientation of your life. Admittedly, that phrase "orientation of your life" sounds vague, but you can get clarity with questions like these:

1. Is your seeking of the Spirit's leading
   a. self-oriented, or
   b. ministry-oriented? In other words, is the Spirit leading you to serve people, to give, to die to yourself, to share the love of Christ with others?
2. Are you
   a. constantly seeking God for your next step, or
   b. obeying what He's already told you? Many people ask God to lead them for their next step but aren't obeying what He's already told them to do.
3. Are you
   a. primarily seeking the leading of the Spirit to enhance your life, make life easier, solve your problems, or give you direction, or
   b. seeking the leading of the Spirit to help you love God and love people?

The principal mark of the leading of the Holy Spirit is to serve others, to love others, to minister to others.

So I learn to be led by the Spirit as I fill my life with the Word of God, which is the language of the Holy Spirit, and as I listen for and follow the leadings and promptings of the Holy Spirit during the course of my everyday life. When I am full of and led by the Spirit of God, just like Jesus, I will serve others. Acts 10:38 reports how: "God anointed Jesus of Nazareth with the Holy Spirit and power, and how he went around doing good . . ." Jesus was a Spirit-led Servant. And just like Jesus, when we are led by the Spirit, He will lead us to serve. We become more like Jesus as we serve, for as Jesus Himself said, "I did not come to be served, but to serve" (see Mark 10:45).

When the New Testament writers picture the leadership of the Holy Spirit in a person's life, they describe the believer as being led to serve others in love. The Holy Spirit is a Servant, and when He is leading in a person's life, they will serve others in love. Paul grasped this as well as anyone. He says to the people of Galatia, "You, my brothers, were called to be free. But do not use your freedom to indulge the sinful nature; rather, serve one another in love . . . live by the Spirit" (Galatians 5:13,16.) In Romans he says, "But now . . . we serve in the new way of the Spirit . . ." (Romans 7:6.) And as we've seen, at the beginning of Jesus' ministry, throughout His ministry, and at the end, Jesus is pictured as serving others in the power of the Spirit.

To be Christlike is to practice Spiritual Breathing as we listen to the promptings of the Holy Spirit, move in the power of the Spirit, and learn to utilize the gifts of the Spirit to serve others. Once again we ask "how?" And once again, just as the Holy Spirit leads us in structured and spontaneous ways, so our serving will be expressed in both planned/structured ways and in prompted/spontaneous ways.

Led by the Spirit in "Planned/Structured" Serving

Every Christ-follower has been saved and filled with the Holy Spirit in order to serve God's kingdom purposes here on earth. God has given every Christian spiritual gifts. Spiritual gifts are abilities given by the Holy Spirit to each Christian to enable them to minister to and serve other people. Serving is dramatically enhanced when I learn to use my spiritual gifts in a way that fits with how God has uniquely wired me.

Paul explains the importance of structured serving in 1 Corinthians 12 when he speaks of the structure of the body of Christ. "The human body has many parts, but the many parts make up only one body. So it is with the body of Christ. All of you together are Christ's body, and each one of you is a separate and necessary part of it" (1 Corinthians 12:12,27). God has designed that the ministry of the local church gets done as individual Christians utilize their gifts to serve. Peter says in 1 Peter 4:10 "that each one should use whatever gift he has received to serve others, faithfully administering God's grace in its various forms." Each one of us needs to find our place of serving in the body of Christ. Then we need to practice serving led by and filled with the Spirit. God will breathe His life and power into our serving as we learn to practice Spiritual Breathing.

One of my primary gifts is preaching. Before every sermon I preach, I pause in my office and ask God to breathe into me His power and love. Preparing the sermon has been a process saturated with prayer as I have listened for His voice in His Word and practiced God-attentiveness, but just before I preach, I pray one last prayer. I want to serve His purposes and serve His people in the sermon. I want the sermon to be an act of worship and love to God. I want His love to flow through me to the people hearing the sermon. So I pray and tell God "I want to love You and I want to love people through this sermon today. I surrender to You once again. May this sermon be an act of loving God, loving people and living surrendered. Breathe into me Your presence and Your words. Fill me with Your Holy Spirit and anoint me to preach Your Word with power, love and clarity."

God wants each of us to discover and utilize our gifts to build up the body of Christ and to find our place to serve in a local body of believers.

In addition to being led by the Spirit to serve in planned/ structured ways, the Spirit will also lead you to serve through promptings and more spontaneous ways.

Led by the Spirit in "Prompted/Spontaneous" Serving

Throughout our day, God will bring people into our lives that He wants us to serve in simple ways. These "unplanned" serving opportunities are often exciting and adventurous. As we learn to cultivate the skills we learned earlier to listen to the Spirit's "promptings" we will hear Him leading us to serve others. Here are a few out of hundreds of possible examples:

- Offering to provide a service (drive them somewhere, mow their lawn, rake their leaves, make them dinner, etc.)
- Joining them in a task they are engaged in
- Volunteering to do a task that's needed
- Praying with someone who has expressed a need

Over and over again throughout my life I have sensed the leading of the Holy Spirit to serve others by speaking to someone, giving money or furniture or groceries to someone, or pursuing a project or idea for ministry. Sometimes it's big and exciting and I marvel at what God has done; other times it feels very quiet and ordinary and no one ever knows except God and me. It's always amazing to me how God will lead me to do something small that reaps incredible benefits later.

When I was planting a church in Kansas, one Christmas our church decided to give me a Christmas bonus gift. As soon as I received it, I sensed the leading of the Holy Spirit to give most of it to a single-parent family down the street. God was prompting me to serve this single-parent family. It was just a simple, quiet prompting, but it was clear as a bell. When we delivered the gift, the mother stood at the door and cried, overwhelmed with gratitude as God provided for her family during a very difficult time in their life. Years later she ended up leading our DivorceCare ministry and eventually became my administrative assistant, serving with excellence in ways that significantly helped our church and me.

There are literally hundreds of opportunities to serve those around us, and the Holy Spirit will call us to serve them with a spontaneous prompting deep in our spirit. Some of the most significant moments of ministry don't happen in the spotlight or platform of organized ministry but in quiet, obedient moments behind the scenes. Ask God to help you be sensitive to these promptings of the Spirit. Embrace your identity as a Spirit-led servant and launch out in the adventure of serving others in the power of the Spirit.

Learning to live surrendered to the Holy Spirit involves embracing my identity as a Spirit-led servant and discovering how I can live out that identity according to how God has uniquely shaped me. I am shaped to serve. Biblical ministry is doing God's work in God's way; it is being in sync with the Spirit of God to know what He is doing and then operating in the anointing of the Spirit to do that ministry.

Breathing Example

As I am writing this book, my son Ryan is in Romania as a part of an eleven country, eleven month missions trip called the World Race run by Adventures in Mission. He's been in South Africa, Swaziland, China, India, and the Philippines, serving the poorest of the poor and being the hands and feet of Christ in orphanages, schools, cities and villages all over the world. Every time he arrives in a new place he breathes out a prayer asking God to "give me love for these people. Help me to know how to serve these people that you love." Without fail God leads him to acts of serving and loving. This morning we skyped together and he told me God has led him to do simple things like playing with kids in an orphanage and more intense things like street witnessing. He is learning to practice Spiritual Breathing by breathing out his fear and breathing in God's love as he pays attention to the leadership of the Holy Spirit. He said, "God speaks to me in the moment a lot, and I just do what He says whether it's to take the time to pray for someone, serve them, give them something to eat or just sit and listen to them." So whether they are doing construction, loving kids in an orphanage, sharing their faith on the streets or digging a ditch, each team member is practicing the skill of learning to listen to and obey the leadership of the Holy Spirit.

Breathing Exercise

God wants to lead us by His Holy Spirit to serve people as Jesus did. He will guide us in both structured and spontaneous ways to serve people. As you practice Spiritual Breathing, pay attention to the breathing in and breathing out cycle, using the natural rhythm of your breathing to focus your prayers.

Here is some language to guide our Spiritual Breathing as Spirit-led servants:

- As we breathe in, we want to receive the Holy Spirit and say: *"Holy Spirit, breathe in me Your power to serve."*

- As we breathe out, we want to remove any sin or toxins and say: *"I confess my inadequacies and pride."*
- As we breathe in again, we want to receive the Holy Spirit and say: *"Holy Spirit, I receive Your power to serve."*
- As we breathe out again, we want to thank God and say: *"Holy Spirit, thank You for Your presence and power."*

Alternate words as we breathe in:

> *"Holy Spirit, breathe in me love for this person"*
> *"Holy Spirit, breathe in me a servant's heart."*
> *"Holy Spirit, breathe in me the attitude of Christ."*
> *"Holy Spirit, breathe in me love, power, and a sound mind."*

Alternate words as we breathe out:

> *"I confess my lack of a servant's heart."*
> *"I confess my serve-me attitude."*
> *"I confess my disobedience."*
> *"I confess my unwillingness to serve."*

Feel free to add, elaborate, or edit as needed. Remember, the Holy Spirit wants to shape our hearts and minds through serving people as He makes us more like Christ. We just need to learn to *breathe.*

CHAPTER TWELVE

The Trust Test

Core Christlike Characteristic: Jesus was a trustworthy steward of God's resources

W ould you say that generally most people can be trusted, or would you say you can't be too careful when dealing with people? Is the average person you come in contact with (who is not your friend or family) someone you view as a trustworthy person?

These questions are at the core of a survey exploring the trustworthiness of people in the United States. It's a fascinating study. The author, Rich Lewis, found out through his research that on average four out of ten people view others as <u>un</u>trustworthy. That means four out of ten people who meet you and do commerce with you are thinking, *I don't trust him; I think she's trying to rip me off. I think he's trying to chisel me out of something. I don't trust her motives.*

Remember, these are not people who know anything about you, so it's not a judgment about you in particular; rather it's a general mindset of distrust. I don't know about you, but that blew me away. (Others of you may be wondering whether or not the survey is trustworthy!)

Lewis says the good news is that that percentage is better than it was twenty or thirty years ago when the United States slipped into the "trough of distrust."

Furthermore, compared to most countries, we're pretty trusting of each other. Only the Scandinavian countries scored higher. We're ahead of all the countries in Asia, Africa, and South America. But even so, when the people in your town wonder whether or not you are trustworthy, 40 percent of them are saying "I don't think so."

The question of trustworthiness is more than a question of interest concerning our country; it is a critical question God is asking every Christ-follower because it is at the heart of what it means to be a fully devoted disciple of Jesus Christ. God is asking each of us, "Can I trust you? What are you doing with what I've given you?" Being a trustworthy steward of God's resources is not a fringe issue but a core characteristic of Christlikeness. Because God cares so much about us being trustworthy stewards, He holds us accountable—something we would be wise to consider.

When Jesus came to earth, He addressed the issue of trustworthiness in many different ways. He taught about it, told stories about it, and posed questions about it to the people around Him. One such example is in Luke 16:10-12 where Jesus says, "Whoever can be trusted with very little can also be trusted with much. And whoever is dishonest with very little will also be dishonest with much. So if you have not been trustworthy in handling worldly wealth, who will trust you with the true riches? And if you have not been trustworthy with someone else's property, who will give you property of your own?" There's a simple principle in these verses: when we are faithful with what God has entrusted to us, He will entrust us with more.

Four Critical Questions

But these verses raise questions for us, four in particular. When Jesus asks "if you have not been trustworthy with someone else's property, who will give you property of your own," whose property is He talking about? The answer to that question will help us understand the answer to the second question: "what is a trustworthy steward?" Thirdly, since I have called this a core Christlike characteristic, it raises the question "how was Christ a trustworthy steward?" If we're trying to be more like Christ it will help us to see how Jesus lived this core characteristic out in His life. Finally, we'll explore "how can I be a trustworthy steward?"

Jesus' phrase from Luke 16:12, being "trustworthy with someone else's property," is at the very center of what this sixth core characteristic of Christlikeness is all about. Jesus is referring to the common occurrence of someone being entrusted with resources—usually money or property—that belong to someone else. The person who is entrusted with the money or property is called a "steward." The "entrusting" creates a relationship between the owner and the steward. The steward doesn't own the resource, they merely manage or "steward" it, and the expectation is that they "steward" in a trustworthy manner.

The biggest key to understanding what a steward is and what a steward does is the word "trust." Stewardship is a trust issue; it's a relationship of trust. The owner entrusts something to the steward. The steward receives a "trust" from the owner; that's why a steward is a trustee. And by definition there's an expectation on the part of the entruster, the owner, that the trustee, the steward, is going to act in a trustworthy manner.

In Luke 16 the "owner" is not named, but the principle Jesus is teaching has an exact parallel between God and us. Throughout the Bible God is pictured as the "owner" and we are the "stewards." God owns everything. Psalm 24:1 says, "The earth is the Lord's, and everything in it, the world, and all who live in it." God expects us to be "trustworthy stewards" of all that belongs to Him. When we ignore that everything belongs to God, squander His resources, or act as if it belongs to us, we are not acting in a trustworthy manner; we are unfaithful stewards. So what does it mean to be a trustworthy steward?

Trustworthy Stewards

Let me begin to answer this question by giving you an example of what a trustworthy steward does *not* look like! Like every other kid growing up, 99 percent of what I used as a kid belonged to my parents. My dad owned everything in our house, including our two cars. He gave me a set of my own keys to use the red Ford Pinto, but it wasn't my car. He was the owner; I was a steward, but unfortunately not a trustworthy one. I raced that car, chased friends down back roads in that car, got chased by the police in that car, skipped school in that car, smoked in that car, jumped railroad tracks to get air in that car, and let my little brother drive on a muddy road, and he wrecked the car. I've actually never written all this down before, and as I see it on the computer screen I am ashamed. That is a picture of an untrustworthy steward. Not only did I use the car as if it were my own, I abused it.

It wasn't until I actually damaged the car that I gave any thought to how the owner of the car, my dad, might feel about how I was using what belonged to him. When it comes to being stewards of what belongs to God, many of us are frightfully like an irresponsible teenager. So what does a trustworthy steward look like?

In order to answer this question, let's look at 1 Peter 4:10: "Each one should use whatever gift he has received to serve others, faithfully administering God's grace in its various forms."

Most of us have jobs or are in organizations where someone serves as an administrator. Depending on the job, the role might be called by a different name, like manager, but the concept is the same: they are entrusted to manage or administer the wishes or orders of the boss or owner or board. It's the exact same idea we saw in Luke 16. In the days of the New Testament this person was called a steward. In fact, the literal words of the phrase "faithfully administering" in the original Greek is "as good stewards."

Peter uses the same language Jesus used in Luke 16 to describe the way we are to handle God's resources. We have been entrusted to manage them according to His wishes or orders. When we manage or steward according to His wishes, we are a trustworthy steward.

So we could answer our second question, "what is a trustworthy steward?" with this definition: trustworthy stewards are those who faithfully manage what belongs to God and has been entrusted to them.

Of course, that leads us to ask "what has God entrusted to us?" According to 1 Peter 4:10 we have been entrusted with, and are to be good stewards of, "God's various kinds of grace." That sounds a little ambiguous and vague, but it is purposely broad for a good reason. The reason is because God's grace is broad; it comes to us in a variety of ways.

I know it's a little crazy, but think of God's grace being poured out like water from a giant showerhead. Now imagine closing off all the holes in the giant showerhead except one. Peter is saying God's grace doesn't come in one small, narrow stream or one narrow way, it comes in manifold, broad, multiple ways. Peter has in mind all that God has graced you with in your life.

This is the second time in verse 10 that Peter has referred to God's grace in broad terms. The first time is in the phrase "whatever gift you have received." The idea is that whatever gifts you have, whatever grace God has poured out onto your life, that is the "whatever gift" that God has given you.

God's Gracings

In the Greek, the word "gift" and the word "grace" are the same root word. This verse is often used to teach on spiritual gifts; each Christian has them and is supposed to use them to serve others. That interpretation is accurate but too narrow. The Greek word translated "gifts" is literally "gracings" or "grace-gifts," meaning "anything God gives us by His grace." This certainly includes spiritual gifts, but it also includes much, much more. Since everything belongs to God, that means everything I have is not really mine but God's. All I am and all I have has been given to me by God, not for me to own but to use and steward in a trustworthy way. All that we have is a "grace gift," a "gracing" from God.

What do you have? Whatever you have is a "gracing," a grace gift from God. This includes your talents, your abilities, your intelligence, your money, your salvation, your kids, your spouse, your house, your car, your TV, your computer, your clothes, your body, your voice, your hands, your mouth, your tongue . . . you get the idea.

You want a wakeup call? Sit down and make a list of everything you "have." Everything. Look at my list above when you get stalled. When you're done, look at the list and say out loud: "This all belongs to God and has been given to me as a trust."

Here's what will happen, I guarantee you, if you will take this experiment seriously and start writing down all of the ways that God's grace has come to you, it'll blow you away and grateful worship will start welling up in your heart. The amount of "gracing" and blessing God has given each of us is overwhelming.

Now, when you're done worshiping, I invite you to think from God's perspective for a moment. God says, "I want to pour out My grace gifts upon people. I'm going to entrust people with spiritual gifts and money and talents. I'm going to entrust churches with the gospel. I'm going to entrust leaders with vision and people and resources. I'm going to entrust individual Christians with My grace, and I'm going to ask them to be trustworthy stewards so My grace gets dispersed to everyone throughout the world." The Holy Spirit is the distributor of God's grace to the church, and the church is to be the distributor of God's grace to the world.

Think from God's perspective how we are doing. The bottom line for a lot of us is that we receive the grace of God and keep it to ourselves. We're mere consumers of the grace of God, not stewards. We tell other people, "Oh, I thank God for His grace in my life," but we rarely consider being a steward of that grace, of all that God has given us. God has gifted us and called us to be faithful stewards of all He has given us.

Jesus told a story of three stewards in Matthew 25. They were all entrusted with grace gifts, in this case money, and expected to fulfill their calling to be trustworthy stewards. Two of them faithfully fulfilled their calling; the third received his money and buried it in the ground. The owner called them each to account and said to the one who received grace gifts but didn't fulfill his calling, "You wicked, lazy servant!" (25:26). But listen to the words he spoke to the trustworthy steward: "Well done, good and faithful servant!"(25:23). Those are the words we want to hear, right?

Jesus was a Trustworthy Steward

After Jesus died, was raised from the dead, and ascended into heaven, He returned to the place He had held for all eternity, the place He had left to fulfill the calling of the Father. No doubt He heard the words He longed to hear from His Father: "Well done, good and faithful Servant!"

The writer to the Hebrews summarized Jesus' life with this same word: "faithful." Hebrews 3:2 says of Jesus, "he was faithful to the one who appointed him." That's why in verse 1 he calls us to "fix your thoughts on Jesus." We want to focus on Jesus because He was faithful, a trustworthy steward of what God had entrusted Him to do.

Jesus got to the end of His life and prayed: "I have brought you glory on earth by completing the work you gave me to do" (John 17:4). Jesus says, "I did what You said. I was faithful. I finished the mission You entrusted to Me." John 19:30 says His last words on the cross were "It is finished." What was finished? Dying? No, much more than that: He finished what God the Father sent Him to do.

We saw in chapter ten how much Jesus referred to the language of being "sent." It's not hard to imagine Jesus recalling God the Father sending Him to earth: "Jesus, I'm sending You, I'm entrusting You, I'm sending You down to earth, and I'm entrusting You with the message of the Good News of My love. I'm entrusting You with My grace. I'm entrusting You with My whole redemptive plan, Jesus, and I'm charging You to be faithful to the calling for which You have been sent."

How was Jesus a trustworthy steward? He was faithful in everything God gave Him to do! This is what the writer is saying in Hebrews 3:2. Inspired by the Holy Spirit, he surveys the life of Jesus and says, "Jesus was faithful in everything God gave Him to do. Jesus was a trustworthy steward."

That's why we describe that faithfulness, that trustworthiness, as a characteristic of people who are becoming like Christ. There's a day coming when all of us will be held accountable by God. All of us will stand before God at the judgment seat, and God will judge us. He'll discern our lives. Just as in the parable Jesus told in Matthew 25, God will hold us accountable with what we did with what He entrusted to us. He will ask: "What did you do with what I gave you? What did you do with the gifts and abilities I gave you, the days I gave you, the strength, the mission, the opportunities, the intelligence, the talents, the influence, the money; what did you do with the resources I gave you?"

If we are honest, few of us feel good about being held accountable in such a manner. So how can we live our lives so that we are trustworthy stewards? How can we live our lives so that we hear "well done, good and faithful servant"? Now that we know what it means and we see how Christ was a trustworthy steward, how can we be trustworthy stewards?

How to be a Trustworthy Steward

The answer is very simple, one small word back in 1 Peter 4:10. We are to use "whatever gift we have received to *serve*, thereby being trustworthy stewards of God's grace." We act as trustworthy stewards when we use what He's entrusted to us to serve others. Instead of being merely consumers of God's gifts and grace, He calls us to use it to serve others. Once we grasp that we are not owners and aren't supposed to be mere consumers, but stewards, we realize that we are to be conduits of God's grace to those around us. God never intended for us to receive His grace and gifts and keep them to ourselves; we are to let His grace flow through us to others. We are distributors of God's grace.

My teenage years were spent in Michigan, and right behind our house was a canal that led to a series of lakes and rivers throughout the region. Theoretically, you could jump in a canoe behind our house and follow the winding canals to lakes which dumped out into more rivers which eventually dumped into Lake Erie, one of the Great Lakes. My brother and I would pack a lunch and follow these canals into lake after lake that spidered out across Michigan. Every time we entered a new lake, we would follow the shoreline of the lake, and sooner or later you'd find there was another river or canal that led to another adventure, another lake, and on and on they went. These little canals served as conduits for the water to flow from lake to lake.

In our adventures, every once in a while we would come to a dead-end pond. Water flowed in but there was no outlet for the water. You could tell instantly that you had reached a dead-end pond because it stunk and was covered with algae. Since the water only flowed into the pond but not out again, the life-giving flow of water stopped and death ensued.

You and I were made to be canals, conduits for the life-giving flow of God's grace to flow into us and *through* us to others. God never intended for us to receive His grace and keep it to ourselves. When we do, we clog His delivery system and the life of God begins to die within us. In southern Israel there's a famous body of water known for having an inlet but no outlet. Maybe you've heard of it; it's called the *Dead Sea*. A trustworthy steward is a conduit of God's grace so it can flow to others. Jesus said, "Freely you have received, freely give" (Matthew 10:8).

So why do so many of us receive God's grace and gifts but then stop the flow, keeping so much of it to ourselves instead of distributing it to others? One reason: *fear*. We are afraid that if we give, we won't have enough. We are afraid the supply will not continue to flow, that it will dry up.

These fears are at their root directed back at God. We are afraid God won't provide for us. Fear is always a lack of trust. We're not sure God can be trusted. This fear lies deep within us; in fact, trust is *the* core issue of life. We want to trust, but fear talks us out of trusting and obeying God. Fear sabotages our desire to be faithful.

Trust is the Core Issue of Life

That's why God teaches us over and over again about trust. It is the core issue of life. God is arranging life to teach us to trust Him. We were made for intimacy and deep relational connection with God. It's the core of who we are. We were made to trust God. We were made to live in a trusting, wonderful, vibrant dependence on God. Stewardship is God's plan to teach us how to trust, to teach us how to grow in faith and faithfulness. Every gift God gives us is a part of His plan to teach us to trust Him.

Here's what I believe. Deep inside each of us, deeper than distrust, deeper than pain, deeper than memory, is the desire to trust. All of life is a battle of who to trust.

We'll never be trustworthy stewards if we're not sure we have a trustworthy God. How you manage God's resources reflects what kind of relationship you have with God, which reveals what you really believe about God, about you, and about life.

At the core of it all is how we perceive God, what we believe about God. All of us have misperceptions of God, caricatures of what He is really like. What we need is a fresh, accurate perception of God. We need to breathe the renewing Spiritual Oxygen of God to restore our ability to trust. There's nothing like getting a taste of God, a reminder of who God really is, to restore our trust in Him. We need to exhale our toxic misperceptions of God and inhale the renewing life-giving oxygen of the Holy Spirit.

We stopped at 1 Peter 4:10, so now let's go back and read verse 11. Just after he challenges us to use whatever we've been given to serve, Peter adds, "If anyone serves, he should do it with the strength God provides."

Peter says, "Don't think for a minute that it's your strength, it's your intelligence, it's your spiritual discipline, that you have what it takes to be a trustworthy steward. No, no, no. If anyone speaks, if anyone serves, they should do it with the strength God provides."

The phrase "with the strength God provides" is the key. Clearly, the strength doesn't come from us; it comes from God. The "strength God provides" is one of the Bible's ways of referring to the Holy Spirit in our life. God's strength is a result of His Spirit in your life. This power of the Holy Spirit to strengthen us is what Paul prayed for the Christians of Ephesus in Ephesians 3:16, "I pray that out of God's glorious riches, he may strengthen you with power through His Spirit." Both Peter and Paul are inviting us to a whole new level of living: operating in the power of the Spirit. The Christlike life cannot be lived in our own strength. We must learn to live in the strength and power of the Holy Spirit.

The Spirit of God is the power of God in us giving us strength. How? Let's look one more time at the parallel of our physical bodies. How do we get the physical strength to move our limbs and walk about in our body? Oxygen-rich blood courses through our muscles, enlivening and enabling them to move our arms and legs and torso. Oxygen breathed into our lungs and distributed to our muscles gives us the strength to move. The same is true spiritually: as we learn to breathe Spiritual Oxygen, God strengthens us from the inside out. The Spirit is the "strength God provides." We want to learn to breathe God's Spiritual Oxygen so we have the strength to live as trustworthy stewards of God's resources.

In fact, the act of breathing in God's Spiritual Oxygen is the primary way of being a trustworthy steward of God's resources. God never intended for us to live the Christian life without breathing in His Spiritual Oxygen. He has provided the Holy Spirit to strengthen us; we just need to breathe.

Breathing Example

Recently, my wife and I felt challenged by God to give something away. God didn't say what, it was just a prompting of the Spirit to give something away. So we prayed and walked through the house looking at furniture and household items. It was so clearly a God breathed prompting that we started to get excited about it. We thought of all the stuff we didn't need, but we felt awkward about giving that, almost like it would be cheating. We came to our living room that had a beautiful couch and love seat and we both looked at each other with this sense of knowing: that was it. It wasn't the nicest thing we owned, but it was very nice. I thought, "why this? We need this furniture. What's the value in giving it away?"

Greed snuck up in my heart and suddenly I felt like a little kid being asked to part with his favorite toy. I didn't want to give away something this nice. But we knew. God was challenging us to steward what belonged to Him and He wanted someone else to have it. So we prayed about who needed a couch and love seat and I asked God to breathe into me His strength and generosity. The excitement began to build. One day Andrea came home and said, "I found the next owner of our couch and love seat!" Then she launched into this story of how she met this woman and as they were talking, the conversation drifted to how this lady felt uncomfortable inviting people over to her house because she didn't have any place for people to sit.

Andrea lit up and said, "we have a beautiful couch and love seat that God told us to give away. We'd love to give it to you." The lady looked at her, stunned.

"What?"

Andrea repeated the story and told her the color of the furniture and assured her it wasn't beat up, but was in fact in very good condition. Tears welled up in her eyes and she just nodded yes. She and Andrea exchanged phone numbers and the next day, she and a friend came over and picked it up. All I can tell you is that God wanted her to have the furniture, but we got the blessing. Only those who give things away know the meaning of Jesus' words, "It is more blessed to give than to receive."

Breathing Exercise

God wants to strengthen us by His Holy Spirit to be trustworthy stewards of all He has given us. He will lead us to use our time, talents, and treasure to serve people in His love. We want to learn to breathe in His Spiritual Oxygen to strengthen us.

As you practice Spiritual Breathing, pay attention to the breathing in and breathing out cycle, using the natural rhythm of your breathing to focus your prayers.

Here is some language to guide our Spiritual Breathing in being trustworthy stewards:

- As we breathe in, we want to receive the Holy Spirit and say: *"Holy Spirit, breathe in me faith to trust You."*
- As we breathe out, we want to remove any sin or toxins and say: *"I confess my fear and greed."*
- As we breathe in again, we want to receive the Holy Spirit and say: *"Holy Spirit, I receive Your strength."*
- As we breathe out again, we want to thank God and say: *"Holy Spirit, thank You for Your grace and power."*

Alternate words as we breathe in:

> *"Holy Spirit, breathe in me Your blessing."*
> *"Holy Spirit, breathe in me a generous spirit."*
> *"Holy Spirit, breathe in me a giving heart."*
> *"Holy Spirit, breathe in me a desire to bless others."*

Alternate words as we breathe out:

> *"I confess my hoarding spirit."*
> *"I confess my fear that You won't provide."*
> *"I confess my trust in money."*
> *"I confess my self-sufficiency."*

Feel free to add, elaborate, or edit as needed. Remember, the Holy Spirit wants to shape our hearts and minds through being trustworthy stewards as He makes us more like Christ. We just need to learn to *breathe.*

CHAPTER THIRTEEN

The Adventure

A couple of years ago I was mired in one of those seasons that prompts books like Lamentations to be written. It was a time of pain and darkness that seemed would never end. I took long walks in the woods with my Chocolate Labrador, Gideon, and poured out my heart to God. Gideon was busy chasing a myriad of smells, but God was listening. One snowy walk in particular I stopped while the sun went down, looking out over a frozen valley, and practiced a simple exercise of Spiritual Breathing. I was exhaling my pain and weariness as I lamented my circumstances and breathing in God's hope, strength, and renewal as I opened my life to His Holy Spirit. Suddenly, as clear as day, I sensed God say "it's time."

I said, "Did you say 'it's time'?"

"Yes, it's time."

"It's time for what? Time to go back to the house? Time to move on? Time for dinner?"

The Spirit just breathed out in a whisper again "it's time."

I've learned to listen patiently and not fill these moments with my words or insistence, so I waited attentively in the cold.

Over the next several minutes, God spoke into four areas in my life where it was time to take a significant step. One of them was in reference to this book you now hold in your hand. I had felt a growing desire and gentle pressure to write for some time, but many other things needed attention, so the book remained just an idea. "It's time," God breathed. "It's time to write the book."

I find it hard to put into words the power and energy that surged through my body at that moment. The air around me was charged with His manifest presence and tears welled up in my eyes as I breathed in His words to me. I lifted my head and basked in the moment while stories, thoughts, and outlines raced through my mind. I wanted to run home and pull out my laptop and write furiously until it was all out, but I just stood there and let God breathe into me His words; I didn't want to miss anything.

Inspired by that episode in the woods, I have felt a divine mandate to write, and now that I am at the end of the book I can see how one of the other words He spoke to me fits in with this book. He also said, "It's time to refocus."

I had begun to let the pain and difficulty subtly distract me from clarity of focus, and graciously, before I strayed much further, God was realigning me, refocusing me. Specifically, He was calling me to refocus on His call on my life to pursue Christlikeness. Leading and preaching and pastoring were important, but I was to lead and preach and pastor toward, and keep a laser-like focus on, Christlikeness. It was His call on my life, the center of the mission of our church, and the subject of this book. But my call to Christlikeness was not an individual call, it was a call in community; I was called to lead this pursuit of Christlikeness and flesh it out in our local church. That leadership adventure has shaped this book.

I have not written a set of theories dreamed up in a dusty library nor described a pipedream of unrealistic spiritual utopia. What you are reading has been worked out in the lives of real people in real settings, facing real challenges. Teaching the truths recorded in this book in the Church of the Open Door in Elyria, Ohio, I have watched God transform our church from a respectable but ailing old church to a vibrant, healthy equipping center for Christlikeness.

I have seen person after person learn to cooperate with the Holy Spirit's work as He is making us more and more like Christ. Countless people have learned how to live connected to God, how to study the Bible and pray; they've learned how to live a life of worship and connect with God through biblical worship. Christlike love is being practiced in more and more relationships. I have seen Christians leave the security of the church building propelled by the love of Christ, reach out and build relationships with lost people, lead them to Christ, and then help them to become more like Christ.

I've watched as our city has shifted its opinion of us from suspicion and avoidance to engagement and partnership. Our church has moved from being ingrown, stagnant, and dying to becoming a life-giving, loving presence in our community through Spirit-led serving. Marriages have been reconciled, the hungry have been fed, orphans have been adopted, widows have been cared for, homes have been repaired, kids have been mentored, and the gospel is being lived out up and down the streets of our region. People come to Christ because they are attracted to Christlike love.

Crime has gone down, neighborhoods have been revitalized, hope has been revived, and unborn babies have been saved. Those previously enslaved by hoarding and fear-based spending have learned to trust God and are living as trustworthy stewards of the resources God has given them. More and more are learning the joy of giving, loving, and serving like Christ. As I write this final chapter, I am more convinced than ever that the only hope for our world is a Christlike church, full of the Spirit, cooperating with what the Spirit is doing today.

Therefore, in this final chapter I want to reveal how this has been worked out in our local church. Jesus never promised to build our individual lives but to build His church. Most of the letters in the New Testament are written to churches, not individuals. All of the calls to holiness and Christlikeness in the Epistles are written to a *group* of Christians, the church, not individual Christians. The Great Commission was given to a group of disciples and is the mission of the *church*. Therefore, every church has the same basic mission: go make disciples. At Open Door, we put it like this:

"Leading People in the Adventure of Becoming Like Christ."

Christlikeness is our goal. Luke 6:40 says that when a disciple is "fully trained, he is like his teacher." Real disciples are people who increasingly live like Jesus Christ. As we cooperate with the Holy Spirit's work in our lives,

God will use all of life to help make us like Christ (Romans 8:28-29). The fruit of the Spirit will mature in our lives, we will increasingly reflect Christ in our lives, and God will be glorified in us.

To help our church more readily grasp the teaching of Christlikeness, I summarized the essential elements into some language that is easier to remember. I want them to be able to remember the Core Characteristics of Christlikeness so they can more fully cooperate with what the Spirit is doing. There's a lot of language in the six phrases, so I arranged the six Core Characteristics of Christlikeness we have explored in the previous chapters into the acronym CHRIST.

Core Characteristics of Christlikeness

Connected to God through the Word and Prayer
Heart of Worship
Relates with Other-Centered Love
Intentional Evangelism
Spirit-led Servant
Trustworthy Steward of God's Resources

Each of the six characteristics has an inter-relatedness to each other that reveals a pattern which can be seen by grouping them by twos. This grouping actually makes it much easier to remember. The first two characteristics (C and H) primarily have to do with Christ's relationship with the Father. These can be summarized by the phrase

Loving God and reflect the Great Commandment as the first priority of life.

The second pair of characteristics (R and I) primarily have to do with Christ's relationship with others. These can be summarized by the phrase ***Loving People*** and reflect the second half of the Great Commandment.

The third pair of characteristics (S and T) primarily have to do with *how* we love God and love people as good stewards of the resources He has given us. These can be summarized by the phrase ***Living Surrendered.***

All the descriptive language of Christlikeness that is captured and represented in the six Core Characteristics can be summarized in these three phrases: ***Loving God, Loving People,*** and ***Living Surrendered.***

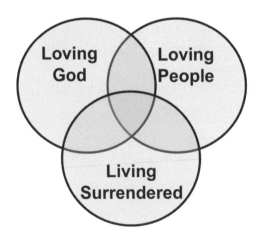

These three phrases could be pictured as three circles or spheres that overlap in our lives. As we practice Spiritual Breathing and cooperate with the Holy Spirit's work of making us more like Christ, over the course of our life these three circles move closer to each other, overlapping more and more until they finally form one circle: there is wholeness, a unity in our lives of loving God, loving people, and living surrendered. We are becoming more and more like Christ and the fragmentation of our lives is transformed into the wholeness and holiness of Christ.

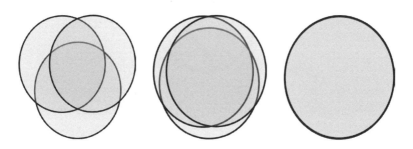

However, our mission is not just "becoming like Christ" but "*leading* people in the adventure of becoming like Christ." We are to become like Christ <u>with</u> others, and in fact we can't become like Christ without others. So it is out of our own pursuit of Christlikeness that we reach out to others and invite them into the adventure of becoming like Christ. Out of the love of God growing in our hearts, we reach out to others. This is our missional pathway, pictured as being centered and driven by a heart of love and characterized by five ongoing steps or stages. This process was illustrated in the ministry of Jesus and explained in more detail in chapter ten. Let me summarize the process here:

We begin "leading people in the adventure of becoming like Christ" as each believer at Open Door who is **Becoming** like Christ begins to **Build** a relationship with a person who is not a Christian. God's love flows through relationships, and it is this building of relationship, this loving investment in another person's life, that opens that person up to the love of God. Building relationships out of love leads to spiritual conversations that directly relate to their spiritual questions and concerns and offer opportunities for us to lovingly share the gospel. These spiritual conversations make it more natural for us to take the next step and seek to **Bring** them to a worship service, LifeGroup, or some event of Open Door that is an environment where they can more readily experience this love and encounter God. We continue to "**Build** and **Bring**" until that person begins to attend regularly. This could take weeks and this could take years; what is important is that we are intentionally reaching out in love to **Build** redemptive relationships with lost people and **Bring** them into an environment where they can experience the life and love of God: the church.

The more they interact with other believers, the more they experience the love of God and start to feel they **Belong**. Throughout this process we are praying and listening to the Holy Spirit and looking for opportunities to share and explain the gospel so they might **Believe** the truth of the gospel, surrender their lives to Christ, and put their faith in Him. This step of faith, **believing**, is what launches them into the **Become** phase. This commitment is in fact their own clear call to begin the journey of Christlikeness in which every step involves **believing** and **becoming**. Here the church helps the believer navigate this adventure of becoming like Christ through a curriculum of classes, ministry experiences, learning of skills, developing attitudes, and growing in the grace and knowledge of God. The core classes in this curriculum are Loving God 101, Loving People101, and Living Surrendered 101. This curriculum is not what makes you Christlike but is designed to assist you in cooperating with God as He uses all of life to make you more like Christ.

As you progress through that process of becoming more Christlike, you begin to grow in love and leadership. These two growth areas of love and leadership combine to move you from the end of the mission statement ("becoming like Christ") back into living out the beginning of it again: "leading people in the adventure." This evidences itself yet again in a life of investing in others by **Building** relationships with them and eventually **Bringing** them to a LifeGroup, a worship service, or some other gathering where they can begin to hear more about and eventually experience and encounter this God who is inviting them to **Believe** and/or **Belong.** At this point they begin their own adventure while you continue on yours, going deeper into the grace and knowledge of God through the shaping of your belief system, **Becoming** more like Christ and then **Building** even more redemptive relationships, eventually **Bringing** them too into the fellowship of the church. The cycle spirals upward, incorporating more and more people in the adventure of becoming more like Christ.

One may enter our church wherever they are in their development. If they are not a Christian they would enter at the arrow representing **Belong** or **Believe.** If they come to Open Door already a Christian, they would enter at **Become.** The current committed Christians at Open Door would enter the process either at **Become** or right into **Build** and **Bring.** Each of the phases is driven by an arrow representing the fact that we never reach a place where we stop growing or moving from one phase to the next. The idea is that we are always moving and helping others move from one phase to the next. We are living out our mission of "leading people in the adventure of becoming like Christ." Each time we reach out and invite people into this adventure, our heart grows larger, the heart of our church for the lost around us grows larger, and the influence of the kingdom of God expands.

This process keeps us eternally occupied with what is most important until Jesus comes again. It is the fulfillment of His last command: to go and make disciples. In fact, there is a rhythm to this heart like our own hearts. There is a natural heartbeat that God has built into every person where blood goes in and blood comes out. This two-cycle rhythm of the heart is reflected in our reaching out and our inviting in. The "becoming like Christ" process is a process of working in and working out our salvation. There is an internal formation and an external expression. We are growing to be more like Christ and we are reaching out to bring more people to Christ. Both have limitless growth potential.

Not only are there always more people to reach with the Good News, there is also endless growth potential within each of us, placed there by the Holy Spirit for us to become more like Christ. We will forever be learning and growing in our loving of God and loving of people. God keeps exposing new areas in our hearts and lives where we need to surrender. Surrender is not a one- or even two- or three-time event. We are to be "living surrendered." There is endless growth potential in each of the six CHRIST characteristics. We have a lifetime of growth potential to develop. Instead of leaving people to develop only in a few preferred areas of interest, we want to help people become fully developed in their Christlikeness. Our goal, like Paul, is to help the church keep "growing in every way more and more like Christ" (Ephesians 4:15 NLT).

What a joy it is to see people move from death to life, from mere church attendance to pursuing Christlikeness, from self-centered living to other-centered loving. Every week in our church I hear stories that illustrate the principles in this book, which of course are simply taken out of the pages of the New Testament. Sometimes I see

Christlikeness in action in such clear ways it brings a tear to my eyes; other times it's simply hearing people use the language of Christlikeness, and I realize they're getting it.

I was at a funeral the other day for a godly man in our church. He had lived out Christlikeness at home, at work, and at church. Everyone respected him and the church was packed as we celebrated his life. Several took turns remembering the legacy he left, including his longtime boss. Then one of his sons made his way to the podium, paused to compose himself, opened his mouth, and said, "My father lived a life of loving God, loving people, and living surrendered better than anyone I have ever known, a gift for which I am grateful beyond words." Overwhelmed, I almost had to leave the room. Tears ambushed my eyes and my heart raced. I wasn't preaching or teaching or vision casting. I was just another person sitting in the audience when the power and simplicity of those words, mirroring the truth spoken by a grieving but grateful son, pierced the heart of each of us sitting in that place. I can't think of a better way to summarize a life well lived. May it be true of you and me as well.

It's time.

It's time for the church to live like Christ.

We just need to learn to breathe.

If you are interested in discovering your next step in becoming like Christ, you may want to try a tool I designed called the Next Step Survey at http://opendoor.tv/nextstep/.

Appendix A

. . . .

Treasure Hunting: How to Discover the Riches of the Bible for Yourself

One of the beefs I had growing up as a Christian in church was that nobody actually taught me how to study the Bible. There are few skills more important in life than learning how to study the Word of God, so I want to take the time to teach you this method right now. It's easy to learn. You can do it. For the next couple of pages, imagine that you and I are sitting down together at a table with our Bibles open. Grab a pen and a cup of your favorite beverage. I want to teach you my version of this process that I have developed and used for over twenty years. I've taught this method to hundreds of people in classes and seminars. It's designed to be easy to use and remember so that you will use it automatically *every time* you read the Bible. In a nutshell this is the process of *drawing out the life-giving truth of the Bible through prayerful study.*

I have written a one-page worksheet on this that you can download at www.JimMindling.com. It might help if you take the time right now to download the worksheet or at least view it as I walk you through this process. I will be referring to the worksheet throughout this section. As I teach you this method of studying your Bible, together we'll walk through a passage so you will learn the skill and apply it immediately. A smaller version of it is pictured in Appendix B.

Ask

There are three phases or steps to this process of drawing out the life-giving truth from the Word of God. The first step is "Ask." You are going to bombard God and His Holy Word with questions: ask, ask, ask, ask, ask. Don't worry about asking God too many questions; He loves it. Jesus said in Matthew 7:7, "Ask and it will be given to you; seek and you will find; knock and the door will be opened to you."

The first thing you want to ask God for is insight. James 1:5 says, "If any of you lacks wisdom, ask God." So the first question we want to ask is, "God, would You open my eyes? I'm asking You, Lord, to give me insight into Your Word." Maybe you want to quote Psalm 119:18: "Open my eyes to see the wonderful truths in Your Law, in Your Word."

This first step is vital, and to help you remember I've placed a small box at the top left-hand side of the worksheet for you to check that you have prayed. Do you see it? Don't skip over this. I wrote my doctoral dissertation on how preachers utilize prayer in preparing their sermons, and in my research I was shocked to discover how many of them prayed about preaching the sermon, prayed for the people who would hear the sermon, but never prayed about understanding the Word upon which the sermon was supposed to be based!

We can't understand the Word of God without the help of the Spirit of God, and it doesn't make much sense to try to understand the Word without consulting its Author. Pray! Ask!

The Holy Spirit *inspired* the Word to be written, He *illuminates* it to open understanding, and He is the best *interpreter* of the Word of God. Ask the Holy Spirit to help you understand, interpret, and apply the Word of God. Ask Him throughout the process. Make your study of the Word a dialogue with its Author. This is how you cooperate with the Spirit. This is the inhale action of Spiritual Breathing. Prayerful study of the Word of God is the only way to rightly divide the Word of truth. As you're praying, read and reread the passage. Read it at least three times. The more times you read it, the better. There's a little box to check that you've done that too, just as a reminder for yourself. (Trust me, it's surprisingly easy to skip these *essential* steps of prayerfully reading and rereading the text.)

As you prayerfully read the text, start asking questions about the passage that you're reading. Don't read it, put it down, and *then* ask questions; *as you're reading it* ask questions. A time-tested way to ask questions is to use what's called the six journalistic questions: who, what, where, why, when, and how? You're using these six questions to do three things: you're *observing, investigating,* and *exploring* what the text says. This is the mindset you want to have as you're bombarding the text with questions.

Let's practice together on Proverbs 2:1-6. Here's how this works: I grabbed one of these worksheets when I was studying Proverbs 2, and I just filled it out. Why not do it with me right now? I checked that I prayed over the passage. And I checked that I read it and reread it and reread it and reread it. I put the Scripture reference up on the top of the page: Proverbs 2:1-6.

Then I started asking the questions. The first journalistic question I often ask is "Who?" Who is speaking in Proverbs 2:1-6? Of course, I believe the answer to this question is always "the Holy Spirit." He inspired these words to be written. But He chose to inspire these words to be written through specific people for specific reasons in specific occasions. So the more I can understand these circumstances and occasions, the easier it will be to understand what the Holy Spirit was saying through these words. As I am asking questions of the text, I am doing it in dialogue with the Holy Spirit. Throughout this process I am asking, "Holy Spirit, what is happening in the text? What are You saying through this passage? I want to breathe in Your Word."

So, in the text, who is identified as speaking? Verses 1-5 don't answer that question so we have to apply one of the most important principles to understanding the Word of God: look at the context. This means you have to look beyond the immediate verses or even beyond this chapter. Sometimes I call this the "neighborhood" that the text is in. The neighborhood, the context, is the verse, verses, and chapters before and after the verses you are studying. So in our case, when we look at the context of Proverbs 2 to find out who is speaking, we keep going back all the way to Proverbs 1:1 where we find that Solomon is the one who is speaking.

In asking the "who" of the text, we want to find out who is speaking, who is writing, who is being written to, and who the main characters are. And so, in this passage, to whom is Solomon writing, or speaking? It's there in the first words of chapter 2: his son, right? So I wrote down on the worksheet next to Who: "Solomon writing to his son."

The next question is "What?" As I read through the text, I began to ask, "Okay, what is he saying?" Well, he's talking about how to find the knowledge of God. So I wrote down "how to find the knowledge of God." This by the way is how I prepare my sermons each week as a pastor. I'm preparing my sermon as I am digging into the Word of God and bombarding it with questions. This is what I do every week. I just open the Bible, I pray, I read, I read, I read, I pray, I read, I ask questions, and then I start filling in the answers to the questions that I ask. The answers become the data that I start praying through. I ask, "What's the big picture that's going on here?"

You will find that not every passage has an answer to each of the six journalistic questions. Furthermore, you don't have to ask them in any particular order, nor do you have to be limited to these questions. I am just giving you the classic starter questions so you know where to start. Honestly though, the vast majority of my questions start with these six journalistic questions.

The next box on your worksheet is Key Words and Phrases. As you're asking questions and observing, you'll start noticing a word or phrase that gets repeated or emphasized. This may be an indication that this is a key word or phrase in the passage. In our Proverbs 2 passage, there is a word that gets repeated three times in these six verses. Do you see what that word is? It's the word "if." And so I circled "if" three times in Proverbs 2:1-5. The repetition helped me notice there's a dynamic that Solomon is setting up here. Three "ifs" followed by the "then" in verse 5 is something worth noticing. When I find an "if-then" statement, I know it often is an indicator of a promise. There's something worth seeing there that I want to uncover. Solomon is saying to his son, "There's a promise I want to teach you: the knowledge of God can be found *if* you will follow these guidelines."

The next thing you can do is not only look at the context, but look to see if this passage has some contrasts in it. See if comparisons are being made in the passage. Look for any conclusions. As I observe these in the text, I write them down on my worksheet. I want to record these observations because I will use what I have discovered in my next step, the "Analyze" step.

Analyze

So step one is "Ask" and step two is "Analyze." Here I want to analyze the information that I've discovered from the questions I've asked and answered in step one. In the classic model of inductive Bible study, I've moved into the interpretation stage. Remember, in every step along the way, I am praying, dialoguing with, breathing in the Holy Spirit. He is the great interpreter of the text, and so I am living in this dialogue with Him as I go through this process. I am praying, "Holy Spirit, open this text to me. What is it saying? What does it mean? What are You saying in this text?" I'm analyzing the text and analyzing the answers to my questions to sort out "what does all of this mean?" In Ask, I want to know *what does it say*; in Analyze, I'm asking *what does it mean?*

The Analyze step has two parts. The first part is you analyze the Scriptures, and the second part is you let the Scriptures analyze you. It's very important that you do both parts. So let's go to part one. You study and analyze the words of the passage and the answers to your questions that you discovered in the Ask step.

There are seven words that start with the letter P that I've uncovered to help me remember how to analyze. As I'm analyzing the Scripture, again, I am praying. **Pray** is the first P. I pray through the whole process. "Holy Spirit, what are You saying here? What does this mean?" I pray and I **ponder**, that's the second P. This is thinking and mulling it over. I'm not in a hurry. I wonder what this is about. I ponder why He said that. I wonder why this is here. God wants us to use our brain and to think. This is the work of pondering.

Sometimes I'll **picture** myself in the setting that the text is in; that's the third P. So as I'm working through Proverbs 2, I might picture myself with my father or a king perhaps, you know, King Solomon, and he's giving me a lesson. Or if I'm in John 15, I might picture myself in a vineyard looking at a vine with its branches loaded with grapes. I'm picturing the branches connected to the vine and the fruit at the end of the branch. I'm putting myself in the passage.

The fourth P is **paraphrase**; this means putting the text in your own words. This is a very powerful exercise because when you have to put the text in your own words, you have to wrestle with it, you have to own it; you have to really enter into the passage. You can't just mimic it. Another helpful exercise is to **personalize** it, the fifth P. I'll talk to myself: "Jim, if you remain in the vine, you're going to bear a lot of fruit." Yeah, I do talk to myself. It will make the text come alive as I put myself in it.

When I get to the end of these five P's, I will often do two more: **point** and **principle**. I will try to summarize the main point in the passage, and I will look for a principle or two that I can draw from the passage. I try to distill all that I've been studying in the Ask and Analyze phases.

As I do these last three P's, personalizing and trying to come up with a main point or a main principle or two, I've already started to move into this next phase of letting God analyze me, letting the Word of God analyze my heart and my mind.

Here I use Psalm 139:23-24 as a guide. I ask God to "search me, know my heart, test me, know my thoughts." I will often say, "Let Your Word be like a lens that the Holy Spirit shines through into my life." I love that picture: the light of the Holy Spirit shining through the Word into my life, searching me, analyzing my heart, my mind, my motives.

This is a powerful time in my life. I will often kneel in my study, and with the Bible open before me I'm asking God, "What does this mean for me? What are You doing in this passage? Open this up to me, Lord. Teach me. I submit myself to Your Word." It's not me, the "master," trying to understand the Word by myself; it's me, the "servant," saying "give me understanding as I submit to Your words and truth in this text." The text is not something that we master as much as it is something that masters us.

Apply

At this point I've already begun to move into step three in our process. The first two steps, Ask and Analyze, prepare us for the third step: Apply. Here, the question I ask is: *how does the text apply to my life?* Studying the Bible without applying it to my life is dangerous. It is actually bad for you to study the Bible for knowledge only. Knowledge is meant to affect the way I live. Paul says in 1 Corinthians 8:1 that "knowledge puffs up."

Knowledge without application lulls us into believing that information equals transformation. In fact, the famous Bible scholar Howard Hendricks said, "To study the Bible to only know what it means is abortion." Whoa, Howard, could you have used a little stronger word? He's saying that studying the Word the right way causes the Word to be birthed in you, and then before it gets a chance to be delivered and to live in your life through application, you stop the life process short. You kill off the power of the Word in your life when you only study to gain knowledge but don't apply it to your life.

The Word must be joined by faith, and we only really *believe* that part of the Bible that we *do*. Lack of application is lack of faith. Jesus referred to this tragedy in the lives of the Pharisees when He said in John 5:39, "You diligently study the Scriptures because you think that by them you possess eternal life. These are the Scriptures that testify about me, yet you refuse to come to me to have life." They studied but never applied what they saw.

James 1:22 says, "Don't merely just listen to the Word and so deceive yourselves; do what it says!" Doing the Word is applying the Word to my life. Years ago I came across an acronym that I use to help me apply the Word to my life. I don't know who to credit this to, it's not mine, but I use it all the time. The acronym is SPACE. I ask the Holy Spirit to make "space" in my life for His Word. I do this by asking five questions, each starting with the successive letters that spell out this word "space." I ask, "In light of what I've just studied and learned in God's Word:

S- Is there a Sin I need to avoid or confess?
P- Is there a Promise I need to claim?
A- Is there an Attitude I need to adopt or change?
C- Is there a Command I need to obey?
E- Is there an Example here for me to follow?

As I ask those SPACE questions, I get better at applying what I've learned in the Ask and Analyze steps to my life. I've been doing this Triple A way of Bible study for so many years it's second nature to me. As you learn this skill of how to study the Bible and practice it every day, pretty soon these steps will lose their rigidity and become second nature to you too. Skills practiced become habits that become life patterns that shape our life. Every one of us has learned behaviors that have become habits that shape our life. As we have seen, Jesus lived in the Word and applied it to His life and it shaped His life. If we want to be like Christ, then we need to learn and practice the skill of "continuing to stay connected to the Word in a life-giving way" until it becomes a habit.

Let me give you four or five ways you can use this Triple A way of Bible study. The first way you can use this is for in-depth Bible study. This is what I do to study the Scriptures for my sermon or any teaching that I want to give from the Word of God. If you're a Bible study teacher, use this method. If you just want to learn the Word of God, you can go as deep as you want. You can spend as much time as you want on this method in one passage. You can study a paragraph, a chapter, a book of the Bible. You can trace a theme through the Bible, like the holiness of God or the holiness in the lives of believers, or the peace God gives, whatever. Do a character study: trace the life of David through the Bible, or Moses, or Barnabas, or Pokereth-Hazzebaim.

Use the Triple A way of Bible study when you read your devotions in the morning. And as you read a portion of the Word every day, apply this three-step method with your worksheet. You can do this with a chapter or one verse. You can do this in a couple of minutes. Take that verse and meditate on it and rip through the three A's, ask what's going on here, who's speaking, what's it about, ponder it, picture it, analyze it, let it analyze you, just kind of savor and soak in that verse all day long, then apply it to your life.

There are many different ways to use this method; it's not a one-size-fits-all deal. Whether you do an in-depth chapter by chapter study, a character study, a theme study, or just take one verse and Triple A it all day, find a way that fits you best. Each of us is in different seasons of life, and what works for one may not work for another. If you're a mother with three little kids, you're going to have a lot less time on your hands than a retired empty-nester.

The Bible never says you have to study the Word for an hour every day. It also never says you have to read a certain amount each day. In fact, it may do less good for you to race through a chapter thinking *I got my spiritual vitamins for the day* than it would have been to take one verse, just one verse, and think about it all day long or all week long. The goal is not to get through the Bible but to get the Bible into you.

I've given you a method; now apply it however it works for you. Go for a walk, take the Bible with you, take a New Testament, or write it on a piece of paper and read that verse. You don't have to do it at a desk. But of course if that is what you prefer, by all means sit down and clear a space for your books, get your worksheet out, and dive into God's Word. Meditate on a verse or two while you're running or working out on an exercise machine. Tape a verse to your mirror, carry it around in your pocket, and pull it out throughout the day, make it your home screen on your phone, whatever. Find what works for you.

Find a way to "stay connected in a life-giving way to the Word." If you do, you will become more like Jesus. As you practice this action of Spiritual Breathing, taking in the Word of God, the Word of God will begin to form your thoughts and influence your thinking and decision making. Living in connection with God through His Word will protect you from sin and strengthen you in temptation. Psalm 119:11 says, "I have hidden your word in my heart that I might not sin against you." Jesus said that one of the roles of the Holy Spirit in the life of His disciples is to "remind you of everything I have said to you." When we fill our hearts and minds with the Word of God, the Holy Spirit will use the Word just when we need it to remind us, to strengthen us, to guide us, and to make us more like Christ.

Connecting With God Through the Word Worksheet

☐ Prayer   ☐ Read and re-read passage   Scripture _____   Date: _____

Ask

		What Does the Text Say?	Notes:
6 Questions	Who? What? Where? Why? When? How?		
Key Words & Phrases			
4 C's	Context: Contrasts: Comparisons: Conclusions:		

Analyze   **What Does the Text Mean?**

6 P's	☐ Pray ☐ Ponder ☐ Picture
	Paraphrase:
	Personalize:
	Points/Principles:

Apply   **How Do I Respond?**

S.P.A.C.E. Questions	Is there a:
	Sin I need to avoid/confess?
	Promise I need to claim?
	Attitude I need to adopt/change?
	Command I need to obey?
	Example I need to follow?